# Legal Deposit and Bibliographical Control in India

# Legal Deposit and Bibliographical Control in India

Prof.A.A.N.Raju

*Formerly Head, Dept. of Library & Information Science,*
*Osmania University, Hyderabad-500 007*

Ess Ess Publications

4837/24, Ansari Road, Darya Ganj,
New Delhi-110002
Tel. : 23260807, 41563444
Fax : 011-41563334
E-mail: info@essessreference.com
www.essessreference.com

**ESS ESS PUBLICATIONS**
4837/24, Ansari Road,
Darya Ganj,
New Delhi-110 002.

Tel.: 23260807, 41563444
Fax: 41563334
E-mail: info@essessreference.com
www.essessreference.com



**Rs.425/-**



**First Published - 2009**

ISBN: 978-81-7000-555-1

Published By Ess Ess Publications and printed at Salasar Imaging Systems

Cover Design by Patch Creative Unit

PRINTED IN INDIA

*Dedicated with deep sense of gratitude to my Doctoral Research Guide Par excellence*
***Prof. (Dr.) M. Radhakrishna Sarma** (1933- )*
*formerly Head, Department of Ancient Indian History, Culture & Archaeology, Osmania University, Hyderabad.*

# CONTENTS

# FOREWORD

India is one of the top seven countries of the world which produce the largest number of books. It is a matter of pride and satisfaction that our intellectual creativity is recognized at international level.

In India there are 24 languages and the number of books published, as per the statistics given by the Federation of Indian Publishers was above 80,000 put together in all the languages. This sense of exactitude which is prevalent in the West was never practiced in India. We just used to say that India publishes a large number of books. Even this 80,000 number does not include thousands of religious books coming out of various Trusts and spiritual organizations which never send their books to the National Library, Kolkata or elsewhere to be counted in the National Bibliography.

To put the matter straight, in 1954 Govt. of India enacted what is called Delivery of Books (Public Libraries) Act which made it mandatory for all publishers to send copies of their newly published books first to National Library of Kolkata to be included in the National Bibliography and then in three more libraries viz. in Chennai, in Mumbai and in Delhi. Even though this has been a law but the penalty for not sticking to this law has been very minimal and a large number of publishers don't conform to the rules of this law. Still a couple of years ago the number of books which reached the National Library, Kolkata to be included in the national bibliography was around 15 to 20 thousand which everyone knew was not the right number. Then, the Federation of Indian Publishers with the help of its constituent language Associations made a count of the books published in various languages and the number increased and as mentioned above it is now over 80,000.

Now, let us see as to the importance of Delivery of the Books (Public Libraries) Act 1954 and the number of books published in a country. It is on the basis of the number of books published that the size and importance of the publishing industry comes to be known to the public and to the government. Only our government can take steps to encourage the industry or if there are any problems to be solved. Therefore, it is desirable that every publisher as soon as comes out with a book or more books should send it to the National Library, Kolkata and elsewhere. This should be part of publisher's first responsibility.

There are a number of other Acts also which apply to the publication of books. The important one is the 'Press and Registration of Books Act, 1867'. This was enacted while the British were ruling over India. Their aim was to know what is being done and out of the copies received they sent one copy to their Londonoffice where full record was kept There was a penalty for not sending copies, which was only Rs.50/- which publishers don't bother.

The author Prof Raju has done detailed research and written a wonderful book which should be read by every publisher and librarian. The detailed tables he has given in the book will prove very useful. He has done his Masters in Library Science and doctorate also.

Having gone through the book, I find that he has done a very good job which was needed to be done. I hope this book will open the eyes of the government and others involved in the maintenance of National Bibliography that a thorough job should be done to know the exact size and nature of books we publish in India.

I commend this book highly and congratulate Prof AAN Raju.

New Delhi
12.09.2008

**D. N. Malhotra**
*President-Emeritus*
*Federation of India Publishers,*
*Chairman, Hind Pocket Books (P) Ltd.*
*J-40, Jor Bagh Lane, New Delhi-110003*

# PREFACE

India's progress, its achievements and failures as well in various fields of human endeavor are communicated through print and non-print media. The published documents emanating from various parts of the country should be properly identified, recorded and made available to the present and future generations without any let or hindrance. There should be a proper mechanism and machinery at local, regional and national levels to have proper identification, control and record of these documents published in various languages and forms year after year. India has emerged as one of the ten largest book producing countries of the world. According to Federation of Publishers and Book Sellers Associations in India, about 60,000 titles are published annually in the country in all Indian languages including English which takes the lion's share.

To have bibliographical control over these publications at the national level requires two operations viz. *1. Production and publication of current national bibliography;* and 2. *Preparation of retrospective bibliographies.* With a view to have bibliographical control over current Indian publications, Government of India has enacted legal deposit legislation in the form of Delivery of Books and Newspapers (Public Libraries) Act, 1954 to institutionalize a system that helps the preservation of country's documentary heritage. The said Act ensures, through compulsory deposit a copy of every publication published in the Country to the National Library at Kolkata and three designated deposit libraries at Delhi, Mumbai and Chennai.

Prior to the enactment DB Act, 1954, and during the British rule in India, the Press and Registration of Books Act, 1867 was enacted to regulate printing presses and newspapers. This Act sowed the seeds for some sort of bibliographical control over Indian Publications. These two Acts viz: PRB Act, 1867 and DB Act, 1954 have contributed the genesis and emergence of legal deposit and bibliographical control in India. But the implementations of provisions of these two Acts were not satisfactory. The National Library at Kolkata and the three designated libraries were receiving between thirty and forty per cent of books published in the Country. Consequently the coverage in the *Indian National Bibliography* is far from satisfactory and not able to reflect the total book production of the country. The reasons for this state of affairs is lack of cooperation from the publishers and laxity in the implementation of provisions of the DB Act, 1954 by the authorities at the National Library.

The working of PRB Act, 1867 is still disappointing in the constituent States of India. Except in Southern States, in most of the States of India there is no proper official machinery worth the name to implement the provisions of the Act.

For the first time an in-depth study has been made on the State of legal deposit and bibliographical control in India, including the receipt of book under DB Act, 1954 at the National Library, the three deposit libraries and also receipt of books from the four southern States at the National Library. The working of PRB Act, 1867 in the States of India and its tardy implementation was also presented.

To achieve effective legal deposit and bibliographical control of Indian Publications suggestions have been made which include among other things a relook on the functioning of PRB Act, 1867 and DB Act, 1954 and recommend suitable amendments by a review committee to be appointed by Government of India.

In the present publication *Legal Deposit and Bibliographical Control in India,* for the first time an in-depth study has been made on the subject, by collecting relevant data. The tables provide for under various chapters throw more light on the present scenario of book production in various languages of India and coverage of subject fields and their receipt at the National Library, Kolkata and the other three designated libraries. The tables also include figures of book production arrived at by the Federation of Indian Publishers and the figures for receipt of books at the National Library which in turn effects the comprehensiveness and total coverage of Indian publications in *Indian National Bibliography.* The vast gap between the figures projected by the Federation of Indian Publishers and the figures provided by the National Library needs to be bridged by effectively implementing DB Act, 1954, by suitably amending certain provisions of the Act.

It is hoped that the present publication will serve as one of the basic sources of information on the subject and go a long way in meeting information requirements of those interested in the subject for further study and research.

*Vinayaka Chaviti*
Hyderabad
September, 03, 2008

**PROF. A. A. N. RAJU**

# ACKNOWLEDGEMENTS

At the outset I would like to thank Prof. M. Radhakrishna Sarma, my Doctoral Research Guide par excellence for acceding to my request of dedicating the present work to him. I would be failing In my duty if I do not thank Sri Dina N. Malhotra, the father of paper back publishing in India who readily agreed to my request and wrote a foreword for this book.

Gathering information on the working of especially PRB Act, 1867 in the States of India had become stupendous task for me. In this endeavor several professional colleagues came to my rescue and helped me to get necessary data. I would like to thank Prof N. R. Satyanarayana, Head, DLIS, Univ. of Lucknow; Prof. Narendra Lakar, Head, DLIS, Gauhati University; Dr. P. C. Shah, Editor, DLIBCOM, Ahmedabad; Dr. Baman Parida, Associate Professor (Retd), Utkal University, Bhubaneshwar, Prof. B. Ramesh Babu, DLIS, Univ. of Madras; Prof. Subir K. Sen, DLIS, Univ. of Kolkata; Ms. Sabita Kundu, Librarian, Techno India College of Technology, Rajarhat, Kolkata; Sri Anand Kelkar, Dy. Director, Directorate of Libraries, Govt. of Maharashtra, Mumbai; who have helped me in getting the required data of their respective States.

Special thanks are due to the Director, National Library, and Sri Syed Abuzar, Asst. Librarian, Sri K.

Sambasiva Rao, Asst. Librarian, National Library, Kolkata for providing the required data on the receipt of books under DB Act, 1954 at the National Library. I would also like to thank Sri K. K. Kochukoshy, Head, Central Reference Library, Kolkata for providing information on *Indian National Bibliography,*

Sri Sumit Sethi, the young and dynamic Chief Executive, M/s Ess Ess Publications, New Delhi, whole heartedly came forward to publish the work. I am extremely thankful to him.

Lastly but not the least I would like to thank and record my sincere appreciations of the support and assistance rendered by Sri M. Madhusudan, who typed numerous drafts and finally the press copy for publication.

— **PROF. A. A. N. RAJU**

# 1
# INTRODUCTION

## INTELLECTUAL OUTPUT

A nation's intellectual output is measured through its publications such as books, journals, magazines, newspapers and other types of reading materials both in print and non-print form. Learned persons and intellectuals from all walks of life communicate their ideas through print and non-print form. These publications reflect the intellectual and cultural heritage of a nation. India with a hoary past and with a billion population and many languages is one of the leading countries of the World in the realm of book publishing. The nation's progress, its achievements and failures in various fields of human endeavor are communicated through the print and non-print media. The published books and other documents emanating from various parts of the country should be properly identified, recorded and made available to the present and future generations without any let or hindrance. It means that there should be a mechanism and machinery at the local, regional and national levels to have proper identification, control and record of those publications emanating from various parts of the Country year after year in various languages and forms. In other words, it is known as bibliographical control and organization of a nation's publication output. The following Chapters and sections and sub-sections deal with various aspects of legal deposit and bibliographical control in India and the laws and institutions concerned with this aspect and the achievements and shortcomings in realizing bibliographical control at the regional as well as at the national levels.

## LEGAL DEPOSIT

Legal deposit is the basis for collection and conservation of information materials published in the Country. It is a statutory obligation which requires the publishers of a country to deposit one or more copies of each publication to a designated agency or agencies as per the provisions of Legal Deposit Law. Lunn defined legal deposit as the "requirement enforceable by law, to deposit with one or more specified agencies copies of publications of all kinds reproduced in any medium or with any process for public distribution, lease or sale"[1]. It ensures preservation and conservation of documentary heritage of a nation and enables the National Library for bringing out National Bibliography and compilation of publishing statistics.

## BIBLIOGRAPHICAL CONTROL

Bibliographical Control (BC) means a system of adequate recording of all forms of information / knowledge materials which add to the sum total of human knowledge. UNESCO defined BC to mean "the mastery over written or published records which is provided by and for the purpose of bibliography. Bibliographical Control is synonymous with "*effective access through bibliographies*". UNESCO has been supporting and encouraging member countries in association with International Federation of Library

Associations and Institutions (IFLA), to have effective control over their publications by bringing out national bibliographies both current and retrospective at regular intervals.

The phrase 'bibliographic control' may present certain difficulties in understanding its scope and connotation. For the purpose of its scope, discussion and presentation in this book, the term 'bibliographic' is defined to include 'books' and other printed materials and the term 'control' is used to describe the procedures where by these materials are systematically identified for the purpose of being able to find them again. According to Doralyn J. Hickey "the combination of 'bibliographic' with 'control', then, will be defined to encompass the procedures devised to identifying all types of materials so that they are capable of being found again"[2].

## UNIVERSAL BIBLIOGRAPHICAL CONTROL (UBC)

Universal Bibliographical Control (UBC) programme is one of the major activities of IFLA launched three decades ago. The major aim of this programme according to Dorothy Anderson was "seeking through standardization in the preparation of bibliographic records and in the machinery for their exchange to build up an international communication system: this is in essence, what we call the UBC (Universal Bibliographic Control) System"[3]. UNESCO has impressed upon the member States in the 1950s especially the developing countries to have National Bibliographic Control (NBC). According to UNESCO, Universal Bibliography is possible only in terms of national units. It advocated the need for every country of the world to establish and maintain an effective current national bibliography which would pave the way for Universal Bibliographic Control (UBC)[4].

## NATIONAL BIBLIOGRAPHICAL CONTROL (NBC)

The phrase National Bibliographical Control (NBC) implies systematic record of all published materials such as books, periodicals and other reading materials including non-book materials published in various languages within the boundaries of a Country. Davidson opined that "a complete national bibliographic Control involves two operations: a) the production of current national bibliography on a regular and continuing basis and b) the preparation of retrospective bibliography of the recorded documents of a period preceding the current national bibliography"[5].

National Bibliographical Control (NBC) is achieved through legal measures. Many countries of the World have enacted laws pertaining to legal deposit, which compels the publishers / printers within the country to legally deposit their publications in designated library / libraries. India has no exception in this regard. It has initiated measures in the path of legal deposite and enacted Delivery of Books and Newspapers (Public Libraries) Act 1954, so as to ensure that the publishers in the Country legally deposit their publications at the National Library, Kolkata and three designated libraries viz. 1) Connemara Public Library, Chennai, 2) Central Library, Mumbai and 3) Delhi Public Library, Delhi.

During the British rule, to regulate the printing presses and newspapers and to keep an eye on the intellectual awakening in the Country, the then Colonial Government enacted the Press and Registration of Books Act (Central Act 25 of 1867). The positive aspects of this Act were to preserve the copies of books and newspapers printed from the year 1867 for posterity and registering them. This Act indirectly contributed to have some sort of bibliographical control over Indian Publications dating from the second half of the 19th Century.[6]

## REGIONAL BIBLIOGRAPHICAL CONTROL (RBC)

Regional Bibliographical Control (RBC) means systematic record of all published materials such as books, periodicals and other reading materials including non-book materials published in the languages and emanating from the region of the Country. For example in the context of India it is the four Southern States of India viz: Andhra Pradesh, Tamilnadu, Karnataka and Kerala.

## REFERENCES

1. Jean Lunn, *Guidelines for Legal Deposit Legislation,* Paris, UNESCO,
2. D. J. Hickey. Bibliographical Control in Theory. *IFLA Journal* V6, N3, 1980. p.234.
3. Dorothy Anderson. Bibliographical Control in Practice. *IFLA Journal* V6, N3, 1980. p.242.
4. UNESCO. The UNESCO Conference on the improvement of Bibliographical Services held in Paris, 7-10 November, 1950. Paris, UNESCO, 1950.
5. D. Davidson. *Bibliographic Control.* London, Clive Bingley, 1987.
6. A. A. N. Raju. The working of Press and Registration of Books Act, 1867 in Andhra Pradesh. In *Study material for Orientation on Press and Registration (of Books) Act,* National Seminar, Nanded, Swami Ramanand Teerth Marathwada University, 2004. p. 151.

# 2

# Book Publishing In India

## THE BEGINNING

A Nation's intellectual output is reflected in the form of manuscripts, printed books, periodicals, magazines and of late in electronic formats. The learned and the scholarly people all over the world right from time immemorial communicated their ideas through their writings for the benefit of the society. India is land of saints, sages and intellectuals and through their writings enriched the intellectual legacy of the Country. Through palm leaves, bhoorja patras and other formats they communicated their ideas to the future generations. The invention of movable printing types by John Gutenberg of Germany in the year 1448 has completely transformed the art and science of printing in Europe and elsewhere and slowly gave raise to the printing and publishing industry in the Western World.

Printing was introduced in India by the Christian missionaries for the propagation of Christianity in India. The credit of introducing printing for the first time goes to Portuguese Missionaries in 1578 in the West of Quilon, Kerala when a Tamil book with Portuguese title *"Doctrine Christian Enlingue Malaumar*

*Tamil*" was published. Since then printing and publishing slowly spread to other parts of the Country. The Christian Missionaries dominated the scene for nearly two centuries until the books on other walks of human endeavor appeared in the 19th Century. Gradually the dawn of 20th Century saw the growth of printing and publishing activity in the Country with the advent of British subsidiaries such as Macmillan (1903), Longman (1906), and Oxford University Press (1912). According to Narendra Kumar "Indian owned publishing firms came to the force [fore] with the political upsurge of the post First World War period. G. A. Natesan of Madras was one of the luminaries of the era. The task of political education was adequately fulfilled through the vast publishing programme of the firm, which justifiably earned considerable reputation through its political tracts, documentary studies and biographies"[1]. The publishing scenario before independence reflected ideological commitment and national freedom movement rather than commercial venture and profit.

## PIONEERS OF INDIAN PUBLISHING

Before independence mostly British and few foreign publishing subsidiaries dominated the Indian publishing scenario. The publishing activity was mostly confined to books in English language. It was only after 1947, slowly but steadily Indian Publishing Houses came into being and contributed to genesis and growth of Indian publishing not only in English but other Indian languages. Foremost among them was Asia Publishing House, Bombay which carved out a prestigious position during the first three decades after 1947, for bringing out scholarly publications in English especially in Social Sciences and Humanities written by eminent Indian authors. To meet the needs of academic institutions this publishing firm has brought out a number of scholarly and useful publications. Most of the books of Dr. S. R. Ranganathan, the father of Library Science in India were brought out by Asia Publishing House. It was said that Indian publishing in the sixties was synonymous with Asia Publishing House. Later on other prominent publishers such as Orient Longman, Allied Publishers, Arnold-Heinmen, Oxford University Press, Macmillan Company of India, S.Chand, Sterling Publishers, D. B. Taraporewala & Sons, Vikas Publishing House, Popular Prakashan, Bharatiya Vidya Bhavan and most of other publishers appeared on the scene and contributed the growth of Indian publishing industry.

In addition to private publishing houses, public sector publishing agencies have also greatly contributed to the growth of Indian Publishing. Mention may be made of the Publications Division of Ministry of Information and Broadcasting, Government of India, Central Sahitya Akademi, Sangeet Natak Akademi and Lalit Kala Akademi, National Book Trust, India, academic institutions such as Universities, Scientific Laboratories, Research Institutions, National Surveying Institutions such as Geological, Botanical, Zoological, Anthropological and Archaeological Survey of India and Survey of India, and scores of Central and State Government Departments and Institutions have contributed to the growth of Indian Publishing through their authentic, scholarly and very valuable publications mostly in English Language.

## INDIAN LANGUAGES PUBLICATIONS

Indian languages publishing also gained momentum after independence and publishers have also emerged on the scene and contributed to the growth of publishing in Indian languages. As for publishing in Hindi was concerned mention may be made of Gita Press of Gorakhpur which has made remarkable reputation in religious publications. Hindi has also held its forte through paper backs. Hind Pocket Books - the Hindi Paperback Publishers have revolutionized the concept of paperback publishing in Indian languages by bringing out several thousand titles and through its *'Home Library Scheme* " it has tried to reach out every literate home. In the words of K. S. Duggal "after a number of half-hearted attempts by several publishers Hind Pocket Books in the North and Seshachalam in the South set out to meet the challenge bravely. The credit of this goes to pioneering efforts of Mr. Dina Nath Malhotra of Delhi and Mr. M. N. Rao of Hyderabad... They organized Home Library Schemes providing every title produced in paperback, appropriate publicity and a fair chance of going to thousands of their members. The 'Gharelu Library Yojana' of Hind Pocket Books ensured initial destination of 15,000 to 20,000 copies of an acceptable title... while Seshachalam has continued to restrict itself to Telugu, Hind Pocket Books starting with Hindi branched off to other languages - Urdu (1965), English (1967) and Punjabi (1972)"[2]. In Kerala Sahitya Pravarthaka Cooperative Society, Kottayam is a unique example of cooperative endeavor for bring out publications in Malayalam and their distribution. In Andhra Pradesh M. Seshachalam & Co. introduced unique *'Home Library Plan'* and brought out a number of low cost publications in Telugu to reach out to every literate home in Andhra Pradesh. The other important publishers who contributed the growth of Telugu Publishing include Adarsha Grandha Mandali,

Vijayawada, Desikavita Mandali, Vijayawada, Bala Saraswati Book Depot, Kurnool, Kondapalli Veera Venkaiah & Sons, Rajahmundry, Addepalli & Co., Rajahmundry, Navodaya Publishers, Vijayawada and Vishalandhra Publishing House, Hyderabad and Vijayawada, Vavilla Ramaswamy Sastri & Sons, Madras, were pioneers in publishing Telugu and Sanskrit classics in the domain of puranas, dramas, prabandhas, kavyas, philosophical and religious books and have greatly enriched Telugu publishing. Of late Vijayawada has became a big Centre for Telugu Publishing. In addition several non-profit voluntary organizations and literary societies also contributed to the development of Telugu Publishing with a sole objective of bringing out moderately priced books of high literary standing and merit. These include Hitakarini Samajam, Rajahmundry, Andhra Saraswat Parishad, Hyderabad, Yuva Bharati, Secunderabad, Desodharaka Grrandha Mandali, Secunderabad and Hyderabad Book Trust[3]. The then three State level Akademies viz: Andhra Pradesh Sahitya Akademi, Sangeeta Nataka Akademi and Lalita Kala Akademi have also published a number of scholarly publications including reference books with moderate and affordable pricing on various aspects of Telugu Language and Literature, Art, Dance, Drama and Music. Telugu Akademi which was established in the year 1968 by the Government of Andhra Pradesh for bringing out College and University level text books and reference books, monographs, and for propagation of Telugu so far published two thousand books in Telugu covering various branches of knowledge[4].

## NUMBER OF PUBLISHERS

There are no authentic sources which can provide

correct facts and figures as to the number of publishers in the Country. According to the *Directory of Indian Publishers* brought out by the Federation of Publishers and Booksellers Associations, there are 11,266 publishers in all languages including English in the year 1973. Of them 1,328 are author publishers. The remaining 9,938 are regular publishers[5]. Narendra Kumar estimated that "there are about 11,000 publishers in the country of which nearly 1000 belong to the corporate sector. They publish 13,000 titles of which, 40% are in English and the other nine Indian Languages which are not listed in the constitution"[6].

According to the *Directory of Indian Publishers* edited by Dinakar Trivedi, the language wise distribution of Indian Publishers is as follows[7]:

| *Language* | *Number of Publishers* |
|---|---|
| Assamese | 118 |
| Bengali | 1,179 |
| English | 1,476 |
| Institutional | 993 |
| Gujarati | 306 |
| Hindi | 2,425 |
| Kannada | 510 |
| Malayalam | 377 |
| Marathi | 666 |
| Oriya | 184 |
| Punjabi | 292 |
| Sanskrit | 383 |
| Sindhi | 28 |
| Tamil | 358 |
| Telugu | 473 |
| Urdu | 596 |
| Total: | 10,364 |

The Institutional Publishers in English denotes academic bodies, research institutions, learned societies and organizations, central government bodies, autonomous organizations financed by Central and State Governments, autonomous bodies like Central and State Universities, Museums, Cultural Organizations and Societies. Mostly these Institutions publish books and other reading material in English and to a limited extent in Hindi and other Indian languages. The National Council of Applied Economic Research (NCAER), New Delhi conducted a survey of Indian Book Industry in 1976 and estimated that "the number of active publishers is in the region of 3,000 of which about a hundred are "large" (fifty titles or more per year), about two hundred are "medium" (twelve to fifty titles per year) and the rest are "small" (five to twelve titles per year)[8].

## PAPERBACKS PUBLISHING IN INDIA

The advent of paperbacks publishing in to the Indian Book Publishing domain was another significant and landmark development. The publication of low priced, mass market paperbacks to meet the ever growing demands of Indian reading community is another important development in the history of book publishing in India. Paperback publishing not only emerged in the English language but also in other Indian languages. Mention may be made of pioneers in paperbacks publishing such as Jaico Books, Orient Paperbacks and Pearl Books in English Language, Hind Pocket Books in Hindi and Emesco Pocket Books in Telugu may be mentioned by way of an example[9]. The year 1958 saw the emergence of Hind Pocket Books pioneered by Dina N. Malhotra who came out with ten beautiful paperbacks at a nominal price of Re1/- each.

This was the beginning of paperback revolution in Hindi Book Publishing. By the year 1965 there were many publishers who came forward for bringing out paperbacks in other Indian languages. The prominent Hindi Paperback Publishers were Star Pocket Books, Asok, Rajkamal, Pracharak, Natraj, etc. Paperback publishing gained momentum in other languages such as Urdu, Gujarati, Punjabi and many other Indian languages[10]. In Telugu Emesco Pocketbooks blazed a new trail and through their Home Library Plan and low priced books touched every literate home in Andhra Pradesh. Visalandhra Publishing House, the household name in Andhra Pradesh also started publishing significant low-priced books and paperbacks dealing with a wide variety of social, political and economic issues[11]

## NUMBER OF PUBLICATIONS

There are no authentic and verifiable sources of information which can provide reliable and correct figures as to the annual book production in the Country. The sources which provide figures pertaining to annual book production in the Country do not reflect the true picture of the country's annual book production in English and other Indian languages. The figures provided by Federation of Publishers and Book Sellers' Association in India based on the figures provided by prominent Indian Publishers mostly dealing with English language publications. The figures do not include the publications brought out by small and author publishers and Indian language publishers. The figures quoted by authors on book publishing in India very much depend upon the statistics provided National Library, Kolkata which was designated as one of the depository libraries and receives one copy of a book and other reading materials published in the Country as per the provisions of Delivery of Books and News Papers Act, 1954. It is well known that National Library does not receive copies of all the books published in India. Therefore, the statistics pertaining to annual book production quoted by authors on book publishing industry in India and national and international agencies is approximate to the actual annual book production in the country.

## BOOK PRODUCTION FIGURES

Right from 1950s, after the enactment of Delivery of Books and Newspapers (Public Libraries) Act, 1954, the National Library, Kolkata has been receiving books published in the Country under the Act. The following figures for a two year period i.e. 1965-66 and 1966-67 will give an idea about the book production both language wise and states wise during the 1960s in the Country.

**Table. Language wise**

| *Language* | *1965-1966* | *1966-1967* |
|---|---|---|
| Assamese | 64 | 118 |
| Bengali | 1,422 | 1,137 |
| English | 10,347 | 9,745 |
| Gujrati | 922 | 1,049 |
| Hindi | 2,376 | 2,767 |
| Kannada | 241 | 380 |
| Kashmiri | 10 | — |
| Malayalam | 573 | 589 |
| Marathi | 1,612 | 1,885 |
| Oriya | 120 | 425 |
| Panjabi | 167 | 142 |
| Sanskrit | 207 | 112 |
| Tamil | 947 | 671 |

| *Language* | *1965-1966* | *1966-1967* |
|---|---|---|
| Telugu | 518 | 538 |
| UJrdu | 372 | 237 |
| Other Languages | 237 | 185 |
| Total: | 20,135 | 19,980 |

**Source:** *National Library, Calcutta*[12].

**Table : State wise**

| *Name of the State* | *1965-1966* | *1966-1967* |
|---|---|---|
| Andaman and Nicobar Islands | 3 | 11 |
| Andhra Pradesh | 1,351 | 712 |
| Assam | 120 | 234 |
| Bihar | 417 | 390 |
| Delhi | 5,900 | 4,310 |
| Goa-DamanDiu | 1 | 46 |
| Gujarat | 699 | 974 |
| Himachal Pradesh | 320 | 74 |
| Jammu & Kashmir | 58 | 14 |
| Kerala | 700 | 771 |
| Madhya Pradesh | 529 | 398 |
| Madras | 1,936 | 2,324 |
| Maharashtra | 3,035 | 3,959 |
| Manipur | 65 | 14 |
| Myhsore | 431 | 673 |
| Nagaland | 4 | 1 |
| Orissa | 446 | 553 |
| Pondicherry | — | 37 |
| Panjab | 670 | 433 |
| Rajasthan | 204 | 310 |
| Tripura | 52 | 21 |
| Uttar Pradesh | 1,118 | 1,224 |
| West Bengal | 3,126 | 297 |
| Total: | 21,185 | 19,780 |

***Source:*** *National Library Calcutta*[13].

During the financial year 1970-71, the National Library, Kolkata received a total number of 18,162 books from States in all languages and 11,617 books from whole Country in language of the State under Delivery of Books (Public Libraries) and Newspapers Act, 1954. The following Table provides break up of these figures.

| *State* | *Language* | *No. of Publications delivered* | | *As percentage of (3)* |
|---|---|---|---|---|
| | | *From State in all Languages* | *From whole Country in language of State* | |
| (1) | (2) | (3) | (4) | (5) |
| Bihar | Hindi | 243 | 2,642 | 46.23 |
| Haryana | -do- | 58 | | |
| Himachal Pradesh | -do- | 54 | | |
| Madhya Pradesh | -do- | 00 | | |
| Rajasthan | -do- | 176 | | |
| Uttal Pradesh | -do- | 1384 | | |
| Delhi | -do- / Panjabi | 3,499 | | |
| Andhra Pradesh | Telugu | 1,328 | 1,253 | 94.35 |
| Assam | Assamese | 368 | 306 | 83.15 |
| Punjab | Punhabi | 560 | 402 | 71.00 |
| Gujarat | Gajarati | 851 | 829 | 97.41 |
| Kerala | Malayalam | 1,063 | 953 | 89.65 |
| Tamilnadu | Tamil | 1,482 | 94 | 60.66 |
| Pondicherry | -do- | 4 | — | — |
| Maharashtra | Marathi | 2,681 | 1,552 | 57.88 |

| (1) | (2) | (3) | (4) | (5) |
|---|---|---|---|---|
| Karnataka | Kannada | 1,391 | 1,170 | 84.11 |
| Orissa | Oriya | 359 | 205 | 57.10 |
| Bengal | Bengali | 2,291 | 1,361 | 59.40 |
| Total: | | 18,162 | 11,617 | 63.96 |

***Source:*** *National Library, Kolkata Annual Report for 1970-71. The above Table was quoted by Samuel Israel in his article "English Language Book Publishing in India. Indian Book Industry. V18, Nos. 5 &6, August-September 1978. p.72.*

According M. N. Rao, who quoted the statistics provided by the Ministry of Education and Social Welfare, Govt. of India, the total number of titles published in India was only 14,064 in 1973. The subject wise breakup was as follows[14].

**Table**

| | |
|---|---|
| Generalities | 309 |
| Philosophy | 400 |
| Religion | 841 |
| Social Sciences | 5,125 |
| Philology | 163 |
| Pure Sciences | 545 |
| Applied Sciences | 1,404 |
| Art | 242 |
| Literature | 4,028 |
| History andGeography | 1,007 |

*The Indian Book Industry,* the official organ of the Federation of Publishers and Book Sellers Associations in India carried out survey of annual book production for the year 1975 and elicited replies from several Indian Publishers of their publications. About forty publishers responded to the survey and a total of 842 new books and 424 new editions were published during

1975[15]. A brief note to the survey states that "it should not construed, however, the IBI vouches for the authenticity of the figures, since they are strictly presented as furnished by the respective publishers"[16].

According to UNESCO statistics for the year 1976 "India is the seventh largest producer of books in the World and ranks third after USA and UK in the production of English Titles". Books are produced not only in English but also in Hindi and fourteen national languages recognized by the Indian Constitution. Abul Hassan furnished the following figures pertaining to books produced in India for three year period i.e. 1973-1975[17].

**Table**

| *Language* | *Number of Titles* | | |
|---|---|---|---|
| | *1973* | *1974* | *1975* |
| Assamese | 259 | 169 | 95 |
| Bengali | 1,140 | 862 | 843 |
| English | 6,183 | 5,501 | 4,800 |
| Gujarati | 630 | 560 | 565 |
| Hindi | 1,814 | 1,368 | 1,697 |
| Kannada | 616 | 394 | 867 |
| Malayalam | 478 | 480 | 430 |
| Marathi | 1,085 | 682 | 1,180 |
| Oriya | 113 | 113 | 321 |
| Panjabi | 138 | 213 | 346 |
| Sanskrit | 54 | 40 | 52 |
| Tamil | 1,089 | 826 | 675 |
| Telugu | 327 | 183 | 255 |
| Urdu | 103 | 195 | 511 |
| Other Languages | 35 | 61 | 71 |
| Total : | 14,064 | 11,647 | 12,708 |

Abul Hassan further states that "these figures

are an underestimate, since information about many titles does not reach the compilers of the Indian national bibliography"[18]. The above table clearly shows that books published in English language takes the lion's share of total annual book production for the three year period. In the year 1975-1976 also, books published in English language constitute fifty percent of the total number of books published. Samuel Israel observed that "thirty years after independence (1947) and after thirty years of promotion and support of Indian languages, English language publishing is, nationally, the dominant sector in Indian Publishing"[19]. The following table provides subject wise figures for annual book production in India for the year 1976.

| Subject Group | Books | Pamphlets | Total |
|---|---|---|---|
| 1. Generalities | 222 | 40 | 262 |
| 2. Philosophy and Psychology | 410 | 9 | 419 |
| 3. Religion | 1,286 | 176 | 1,462 |
| 4. Sociology | 516 | 10 | 26 |
| 5. Political Science | 1,96 | 31 | 1,998 |
| 6. Law, Public Administration | 618 | 439 | 1,057 |
| 7. Military Science | 12 | - | 12 |
| 8. Education | 290 | 11 | 301 |
| 9. Trade, Communications | 237 | 23 | 249 |
| 10. Folklore, Ethnography | 134 | — | 134 |
| 11. Linguistics | 258 | 3 | 261 |
| 12. Mathematics | 133 | 44 | 137 |
| 13. Natural Sciences | 608 | 8 | 616 |
| 14. Medical Sciences | 198 | 7 | 205 |
| 15. Technology | 526 | 915 | 1,441 |
| 16. Agriculture, Forestry | 264 | 10 | 274 |
| 17. Domestic Science | 110 | 6 | 116 |
| 18. Commerce | 103 | — | 103 |

| Subject Group | Books | Pamphlets | Total |
|---|---|---|---|
| 19. Architecture, Town Planning, the Arts | 187 | 6 | 193 |
| 20. Games and Pastimes | 125 | 8 | 133 |
| 21. Literature | 4,792 | 9 | 4,801 |
| 22. Geography, Travel | 239 | 10 | 249 |
| 23. History, Geography | 847 | 6 | 853 |
| Total: | 14,082 | 1,720 | 15,802 |

***Source:*** *Compiled from National Library data andquoted by Samuel Israel in his article titled* 'English Language Book Publishing in India'. *Indian Book Industry,* V18. Nos. 5 & 6, August & Sept. 1978. p.73.

Samuel Israel further states that under notes 1 below the above Table that "it is estimated by a knowledgeable librarian that some fifty per cent of books published in India are not submitted to the three legal deposit libraries, among which the National Library, Calcutta, is charged with the preparation of *Indian National Bibliography and Compilation of Statistics*"[20]. As per the observation of "knowledgeable Librarian" and as quoted by Samuel Israel that "fifty per cent of books are not submitted to the designated depository libraries" one can conclude that the above Table do not reflect the actual annual book production in the country in English and other Indian languages in India. Lokanath Bhatacharya observed that "there is a near absence of statistical data in India in quite a vital fields including the subject of the present publication"[21].[Books and Reading]. The following Table gives us an idea of receipt of books at the National Library, Kolkata for the years 1980-1982[22].

**Table : Language wise receipt of books**

| *Language* | *Number of Titles* | | |
|---|---|---|---|
| | *1981* | *1982* | *1983* |
| Assamese | 101 | 80 | 117 |
| Bengali | 888 | 965 | 834 |
| English | 5,5895 | 5,145 | 4,313 |
| Gujarati | 724 | 645 | 726 |
| Hindi | 1,379 | 1,276 | 1,221 |
| Kannada | 751 | — | 468 |
| Malayalam | 772 | 552 | 443 |
| Marathi | 1,292 | 1,12 | 1,134 |
| Oriya | 442 | 127 | 15 |
| Panjabi | 308 | 325 | 308 |
| Sanskrit | 20 | 15 | 36 |
| Tamil | 549 | 787 | 548 |
| Telugu | 167 | 355 | 309 |
| Urdu | 142 | 155 | 146 |
| Other Languages | 27 | 23 | 31 |
| Total: | 13.157 | 11, 562 | 10,649 |

It appears that the main source for book production statistics of Indian Publications are concerned, it is the National Library, Kolkata and one has to depend upon this source for analyzing and writing on book production in India. It is pretty well known that National Library, Kolkata receives only 30% to 40% per cent of Indian publications under DB Act, 1954. There are no other 'authentic' and official sources which can provide reliable figures on book production in India. The Statistics provided by Federation Indian Publishers are only approximate figures and may not reflect the true and actual annual book production in India.

## Federation of Indian Publishers figures

During the last six decades, after independence, Indian Publishing has come a long way. The growth of education at all levels, the increase in literacy percentage, the establishment of schools, colleges, universities, R & D Institutions, learned societies, the increase in the enrollment of educational institutions, Central and State Governments support for growth of education has indirectly contributed for the demand for books and reading materials both in print and non-print media. The emergence of Indian Publishing Industry to meet the intellectual needs of the Country is another important factor and a mile stone and transformed India as "one of the top six publishing countries of the world". The two publications brought out by Federation of Indian Publishers viz. *1) 50 YEARS of Book Publishing in India* and *2) 60 years of Book Publishing in India, 1947-2007, BOTH EDITED BY THE DOYEN OF PAPERBACK REVOLUTION IN INDIA, D. N. MALHOTRA PROVIDES FIGURES FOR ANNUAL BOOK PRODUCTION IN INDIA.*

D. N. Malhotra, the editor of *50 years of Book Publishing in India since independence* states that the "newly computed figures give a total of over 60,000 books published in India annually and the exact figure for the year 1997 has been established at 57,386 for books published in all Indian languages including English"[23]. The language wise break up of the books is as follows:

| | |
|---|---|
| Assamese | 1,019 |
| Bengali | 4,286 |
| English | 12,528 |
| Gujarati | 2,462 |
| Hindi | 10,026 |

| | |
|---|---|
| Kannada | 1,500 |
| Malayalam | 2,573 |
| Marathi | 4,259 |
| Oriya | 597 |
| Punjabi | 1,024 |
| Sanskrit | 585 |
| Tamil | 5,879 |
| Telugu | 2,687 |
| Urdu | 1,626 |
| Kashmiri | 85 |
| Dogri | 54 |
| Konkani | 84 |
| Sindhi | 112 |
| Total: | 57,386 |

The above statistics were collected by the Federation through its associates in Indian Languages Publishers Associations in the Country.

In the present century i.e. 21st Century the scenario of Indian publishing has been changed for the better. According to D. N. Malhotra editor of *60 years of Book Publishing in India 1947-2007* "the total publishing scene in India which comprises around 80,000 new books a year published in 24 languages. The job is actively performed by 16,000 publishers"[24]. He further states that "the largest number of books are published in Hindi i.e., about 25 per cent of the total publishing done in all the languages. It is followed by English, and then if we make a group of 6 languages i.e. Bengali, Malayalam, Marathi, Gujarati, Tamil and Telugu, this group comes second. After that the other 5 languages if we club them together on the basis of number of books published in them, these would be Assamese, Kannada, Oriya, Punjabi and Urdu. Following group are 4 languages i.e. Kashmiri, Dogri,

Konkani and Sindhi. The last one to be dealt with is Sanskrit[25]. The following Table provides figures for books published in major Indian languages for the year 2004.

**Table**

| *Name of the Language:* | *No. of books published In 2004* |
|---|---|
| Assamese | 1,285 |
| Bengali | 5,538 |
| English | 18,752 |
| Gujarati | 3,213 |
| Hindi | 21,370 |
| Kannada | 1,998 |
| Malayalam | 3,358 |
| Marathi | 5,475 |
| Oriya | 763 |
| Punjabi | 1,298 |
| Sanskrit | 749 |
| Tamil | 7,525 |
| Telugu | 3,482 |
| Urdu | 2,172 |
| Kashmiri | 140 |
| Dogri | 105 |
| Konkani | 138 |
| Sindhi | 176 |
| Other languages including folk literature, religious books, etc. | 5,000 |
| Total: | 82,537 |

***Source:*** *D. N. Malhotra, Ed. 60 years of book publishing in India,* 1947-2007. (New Delhi, The Federation of Indian Publishers, 2006) p. 12.

## PRB ACT, 1867

As per the provisions of the Press and Registration of Books Act, 1867, every Printer in the states of India has to submit certain copies, as per the rules framed by the respective State Governments, to the designated agency for record and preservation. For example in Andhra Pradesh, the Registrar of Publications, Govt. of Andhra Pradesh is the designated agency which receives 3 copies of each and every publication from the printers in the State. The said Act is not vigorously implemented in other States of India. In most of the States there is no machinery to implement the provisions of the Act. The provisions of the Act indirectly support the concept of legal deposit in India even though there is a specific law i.e., the Delivery of Books and News Papers Act, 1954 which takes care of legal deposit in India. As an example the following table provides figures for the receipt of books in Andhra Pradesh as per the provisions of PRB Act, 1867, for the year 1997-98.

In Andhra Pradesh a total of 650 books and 365 periodical titles were published during the year 1997-98[26]. The following Table provides language wise breakup of books and periodicals.

| *S.No.* | *Language* | *Books* | *Periodicals(Titles)* |
|---|---|---|---|
| 1 | Telugu | 437 | 258 |
| 2 | Hindi | 22 | 6 |
| 3 | Urdu | 36 | 29 |
| 4 | Sanskrit | — | — |
| 5 | Tamil | 2 | 1 |
| 6 | Kannada | 3 | 1 |
| 7 | Marathi | — | — |
| 8 | English | 141 | 67 |
| 9 | Bilingual & Polyglot | 9 | 3 |
| | | 650 | 365 |

The above figures may not reflect the actual annual book production in Andhra Pradesh. These figures were obtained from the office of Registrar of Publication, Government of Andhra Pradesh, which receives 3 copies of each printed book from the printers in the State, as per the provisions of Press and Registration of Books Act, 1867. It is open secret that majority of printers in the State do not comply with the provisions of the Act. The same may true with the Printers of other States of Indian Union.

The succeeding Chapters of this book deal with the legal deposit and bibliographical control in Indian and working PRB Act, 1867 and DB Act 1954 in the backdrop of annual book production in India as per the figures provided the Federation of Indian Publishers and the receipt of books at the National Library, Kolkata and other three designated libraries at Delhi, Mumbai and Chennai, as per the provisions of DB Act, 1954. There is gap between the number of books received at the National Library and other three designated libraries and the figures provided by the Federation of India Publishers. The fact is that legal deposit and bibliographical control in India and its realization suffers from various known and unknown factors. The succeeding chapters deal with this aspect briefly with available facts and figures.

## REFERENCES


1. Narendra Kumar. Truth about Indian Publishing. *Indian Book Industry*, v14,Nos.5&6, August-September, 1976. p.45.
2. K. S. Duggal. The Mass Circulation Books. *Indian Book Industry*. V15,N3, Dec. 1976, p. 12.
3. K. B. Satyanarayana. Telugu Publishing and its Bibliographical Control. *InNational Bibliographical Control: Problems and Perspectives*. Ed. by A. A. N. Raju and L. S. Ramaiah, New Delhi, Allied Publishers, 2003. p.138.
4. G. Narayana Rao. Telugu Akademi. *Andhra Jyoti* Sunday supplement. Feb.24, 2008. p. 10.

5. Quoted by M. N. Rao in *The Book Publishing Manual,* prepared by M. N. Rao, New Delhi. The Federation of Publishers and Booksellers Associations in India. 1974. pp. 11 -12.
6. Narendra Kumar. Opcit. p.46.
7. Dinakar Trivedi, Ed. *Directory of Indian Publishers,* New Delhi: The Federation of Publishers and Book Sellers Association in India. 1973.
8. Quoted by Samuel Israel under notes 3 in his article titled "English Language Book Publishing in India". *Indian Book Industry.* V.18, Nos.5 & 6. August-Sept. 1976. p.75.
9. M.N. Rao. *The Book Publishing Manual.* New Delhi; The Federation of Publishers and Booksellers Association in India, 1974. p.9.
10. Amarnath. Paper books: A Revolution in India. *Indian Book Industry.* V.15,N3, Dec. 1976. p. 17.
11. K. B. Satyanarayana. Telugu Publishing and its Bibliographical Control. In *National Bibliographical Control: Problems and Perspectives,* Ed. by A. A. N. Raju and L. S. Ramaiah, New Delhi. Allied Publishers, 2003, p. 138.
12. The Figures were quoted by S. K. Mukherjee in his book *Development of Libraries and Library Science in India.* Calcutta, the Word Press, 1969 p.250.
13. The above figures were quoted b y S. K. Mukherjee in his book: *Development of Libraries and Library Science in India* Calcutta, The Word Press 1969, p.259.
14. Quoted by M. N. Rao. Opcit. P.12.
15. Book Production in India 1975 - IBI Survey Report: *Indian Book Industry,* V.13, Nos. 3 & 4 Dec. 75. Jan. 76, p.73.
16. Ibid. p.73.
17. Abul Hassan. Indian Book Industry - Some salient Features. *Indian Book Industry,* V14, Nos. 5 & 6, August-Sept. 1976. p.41. (The basic source for the above figures is National Library, Kolkata).
18. Abul Hassan, Ibid, p.41.
19. Samuel Israel. English Language Book Publishing in India. *Indian Book Industry,* V18, Nos. 5 & 6, August-Sept. 1978. p.59.
20. Samuel Israel, opcit. P.73.
21. Lokanath Bhattacharya. *Books and Reading in India.* Paris,

UNESCO, 1986. p.57.

22. Ibid. p.60 [Source: National Library, Kolkata].
23. D. N. Malhotra. *Ed.* 50 *years of Book Publishing in India since Independence* New Delhi, Federation of Indian Publishers,1998, P.12.
24. D. N. Malhotra, Ed. *60 years of Book Publishing in India,* 1947-2007. (New Delhi, Federation of Indian Publishers, 2006) pp.13-14.
25. Ibid., p.14.
26. 44th All India Library Conference of the Indian Library Association, Feb.25-28, 1999. Hyderabad *Souvenir,* Hyderabad, Academy of Library Science and Documentation, Hyderabad and Potti Sree Ramulu Telugu University, Hyderabad, 1999. p.33.

# 3
# LEGAL DEPOSIT IN INDIA

## LEGAL DEPOSIT

India with many languages including English as a language of higher education, research and state administration has emerged as one of the ten largest book producing countries of the World. According to Federation of Publishers and Book Sellers Associations in India, about 60,000 titles are published annually in the Country in all the Indian languages including English which takes the lion's share.

Anuradha S. Chagti opines that "India as per the data provided by the International Publishers Association is among the 7th largest publishing nation in the world. It publishes about 60,000 to 70,000 titles in the year. Books are published in 18 languages by about 11,000 publishers through out the country. In English language we are the third largest publishers in the world after UK and US"[1]. But there are no authentic sources which can provide actual annual production in the country. The only 'official source' available are the Annual Reports of the National Library, Kolkata, which provide figures of the receipt of books published in our country under the provisions of Delivery of Books and Newspapers (Public Libraries) Act, 1954. But it is open secret that the National Library does not get all the publications published in the Country.

To have bibliographic control over these publications at the national level it requires two operations viz: 1. Production and Publication of current national bibliography on a regular and continuous basis, and 2. Preparation of retrospective bibliographies. With a view to have bibliographical control over current publications many countries the World over have enacted legal deposit legislation and established national bibliographical agencies to bring out current national bibliographies. UNESCO and IFLA have played a prominent role in the spread of the concept of Universal and National Bibliographical Control and assisted the member countries especially developing countries by providing expertise and material assistance as well to realize the concept of national bibliographical control.

Luhn defined legal deposit as "the requirement enforceable by law, to deposit with one or more specified agencies copies of publications of all kinds reproduced in any medium or with any process for public distribution, lease or sale"[2]. It is a means by which a comprehensive and valuable intellectual output of the nation in the form of books and reading materials is collected together as record of nation's published heritage. It is enforced by law and every publisher in the country has to deposit copies of their publications to one or more designated libraries. The books so collected are conserved and preserved for the benefit of present and future generations as national documentary heritage.

P. J. Lor opined that "legal deposit legislation is

important to national libraries because legal deposit can provide the basis for the collection and conservation of information materials published in the country, and further, for their bibliographic description and physical availability. It is therefore relevant to the exercise of heritage-related functions. In addition, legal deposit may assist the National Library in compiling National Publishing Statistics"[3].

Bandyopadhyay[4] states that legal deposit serves four major purposes which are as follows:

1. "It helps put copyright legislation into effect. The author or any other copyright holder has the right to safeguard his right in the publication.
2. It ensures preservation of material being produced ontemporaneously for posterity...
3. In some countries it acts as the signal for explicit authorization for the publication of the work deposited...
4. It helps produce comprehensive national bibliography without needing any search into diverse sources for its presentation".

## ORIGIN OF LEGAL DEPOSIT IN INDIA

Legal deposit in India had its genesis with the passing of the Delivery of Books and Newspapers (Public Libraries) Act, 1954 to institutionalize a system that helps the preservation of the Country's cultural and intellectual heritage embodied in documents. The said Act ensures total coverage through compulsory deposit of a copy of every publication published within the Country to the National Library at Kolkta and three designated libraries. The said Act under section 3 states that "... publisher of every book published in the territories to which this Act extends after the commencement of this Act, shall not withstanding any agreement to the contrary, deliver at his own expense a copy of the book to the National Library at Calcutta and one such copy to each of the other three public libraries within thirty days from the date of its publication".

Section 3A specifies that "...The Publisher of every newspaper, published in the territories to which this Act extends, shall deliver at his own expense one copy of each issue of such newspaper as soon as it is published to each public library as may be notified in this behalf by the Central Government in the Official Gazette". Section 5 states that "Any publisher who contravenes any provision of this Act or any rule made there under shall be punishable with fine which may extend to fifty rupees..."

Publishing industry in the country has gone a long way during the past five decades since the enactment of DB Act in 1954. Bandyopadhyay opines that "the publication industry has expanded enormously in terms of range of subjects' covered and total number of titles appearing in these subjects. Publication in regional languages have risen in an increasing proportion, even as English remains the predominant language of publication in the country followed closely by Hindi. Also a wide range of quality publications are being brought out every year in the regional languages"[5].

According to Abuzar "Publishing [in India] has now become an industry in organized as well as unorganized sectors... Bibliographic Control over this enormous publishing situation is difficult. There is no organization which can give a comprehensive and reliable figure of book publishing in a year. The history of National Bibliographic Control in India has proved to be a game of hide and seek between the publishers/ printers and legal deposit Acts"[6].

## SOUTH INDIA SCENARIO

South India or Southern Region of India consisting of the States of: Andhra Pradesh, Tamilnadu, Karnataka and Kerala played a prominent role in the history of the Country and its emergence as a nation. The Southern States of India are rich in history, art and architecture, tradition and culture, religion and philosophy, languages and literatures and folklore carved out a distinct and prominent place in the history of entire Country[7]. The region has carved out a niche in respect of learned and educational institutions functioning in various parts of South India. Leading Publishers in the State Capital cities like Chennai, Bangalore, Hyderabad, Trivandrum and other metropolitan Centres such as: Madurai, Coimbatore, Vijayawada, Visakhapatnam, Mysore, Mangalore, Kochi and Thrissur have greatly contributed to the growth of publishing industry in the region. During the last two decades many author-publishers have also emerged on the scene and contributed to the growth of publication activity in Southern India.

## LEGAL DEPOSIT GUIDELINES

Legal deposit ensures efficient means of building up of nation's print and non-print material collection for preservation and conservation for posterity. Legal deposit legislation is means by which the national governments build book and non-book collections in designated libraries to become depositories of a country's documentary heritage and making available this heritage to the present and future generations. It enables every citizen to have access to the nation's publishing output and there by meets the intellectual needs of the society at large. *The Guidelines for Legal Deposit Legislation*[8] brought out UNESCO provides legal frameworks for a national legal deposit scheme in print form and these are presented below for information. These points cover: *1. Basic Principles, 2. Legislation, 3. Elements of Legal Deposit, 4. Object of Legal Deposit, 5. Electronic Publications.*

## 1. BASIC PRINCIPLES

1.1. Legal deposit should be a statutory obligation. While feasible, a voluntary deposit system is not recommended.

1.2. Legal deposit should be established as a national responsibility. This principle should not prevent other jurisdictions within the national entity from developing their own internal legal deposit system if they have the legislative power to do so.

1.3. The national deposit collection should be the property of the State, and the depository should make every possible effort to keep the material received on deposit, considering its preservation responsibility.

1.4. Legal deposit should be based on the principle that any published material, in its broadest sense, that is made available to the public is subject to deposit unless specifically excluded in the law.

1.5. No compensation, financial or otherwise, should be granted to depositors.

1.6. Access to legal deposit collections should be free, both on the premises and through interlibrary loans. The request of reasonable administrative fees should not be considered as a breach of this principle.

1.7. The copyright act might need to be amended in order to allow reproduction of protected work for long-term preservation purposes. The derogation clause, while always feasible, is not recommended.

## 2. LEGISLATION

2.1. The legislation could be a separate legal deposit law or part of another law, such as the national library act. If it is decided to make the legislation part of the copyright act, it should be made clear that there is no direct link between the deposit of copies and the granting of the copyright.

2.2. The act should reflect all basic principles.

2.3. The objectives of legal deposit should be clearly stated in the law.

2.4. The law requiring legal deposit should be enforceable and include a fine structure for non-compliance.

2.5. The language of the law should be clear, accurate, concise and easy to read. Ambiguity and vagueness should be avoided.

2.6. The law should include clear definitions of the terms used in order to ensure that the intent of the legislator is understood.

## 3. ELEMENS OF LEGAL DEPOSIT

### 3.1. Origin of the publication

The origin or place of publication of each item should be the basic consideration of any legal deposit scheme. Authors, publishers, producers, distributors, printers and importers may be required to deposit copies.

Since a national law cannot be applied on an extraterritorial basis, material published or produced abroad by national citizens and publishers should be deposited on a voluntary basis by them or acquired through traditional acquisition means.

For on-line electronic publications, the publication source should be identified by using the geographic location of the publishing or producing organization or individual.

## 3.2. Comprehensiveness

**3.2.1.** The definition of the material to be deposited should be as broad as possible in order to include all types of information carriers Independent of the format.

**3.2.2.** All types of print material as well as audio-visual documents should be subject to legal deposit. Broadcast material, both radio and television should be subject to legal deposit. The legislation should also cover electronic publications, both off-line and on-line, including multimedia networked publications, even if the national legal deposit agency is not yet in a position to collect such material. In this area, the law should remain as general as possible since technology evolves rapidly.

**3.2.3.** The basic criteria for being an object of legal deposit should be that the material is produced in multiple copies and made available to the public.

*3.2.3.1.* For on-line electronic publications, as well as radio and television programs, the only criterion should be accessibility to the public.

**3.2.4.** A legal deposit law should not be retroactive and the material published / produced prior to the entry into force of the law should be collected through voluntary deposit or traditional acquisition means.

**3.2.5.** Legal deposit legislation should be neural as far as content of the material to b e deposited is concerned. Therefore, any type of material corresponding to the basic criteria should be deposited disregarding any value judgment of the material, should it be of a moral, political, artistic or literary nature.

## 3.3. Depositor

**3.3.1.** The depositor should be the organization or the individual responsible for publishing / producing and making available the copies of a document. If it is decided to assign the deposit responsibility to the owner of the copyright, the law should be very explicit and clear on this matter. With on-line material since there will be more and more individuals "publishing" or "producing" their own material, the legislation should include them as depositor.

## 3.4. Depository

**3.4.1.** The national library of the country, or any other national institution playing a similar role, should be the depository. Legal deposit may also be decentralized and involve other national agencies as depositories for more specialized material. In that case, there should be a statutory mechanism for the co-ordination of the various agencies responsible for legal deposit, and measures should be adopted to ensure that users have seamless access to the national published heritage in all media.

## 3.5. Number of Copies

**3.5.1.** At a minimum, two copies should be deposited, one for preservation and the other for use. But this number could vary depending on the national objectives of the scheme.

**3.5.2.** There could be an exception for certain types of material that is more expensive to produce and / or for which the market is more limited. In such cases, only one copy could be deposited.

**3.5.3.** For electronic publications, the issue of the number of copies is replaced by the issue of the number of concurrent users of the product. The law should make it compulsory for the publisher / producer to provide access to a minimum of one user at a time.

### 3.6. Time of Deposit

**3.6.1.** There is no standard to follow, except that it should be as soon as possible after publication, preferably within one week but not later than four weeks.

## 4. OBJECT OF LEGAL DEPOSIT

### 4.1. Books

**4.1.1.** Books represent the basic object of legal deposit. The definition of what constitutes a book has to appear in the law and should be clear. Inclusions and exclusions should be defined. The minimum number of pages required and the minimum number of copies printed should be determined by the regulations.

The law should also specify that variations of a book, whether variations of content (other editions), language (translations) or form (trade, deluxe, pocket editions), should be deposited.

**4.1.2.** Books also published in electronic format, whether off-line or on-line should be deposited. The way such material will be accessed should be carefully looked at in order to respect the requirements of international conventions.

**4.1.3.** Only the first printing of a book must be deposited, unless further printings have a different physical presentation.

**4.1.4.** All accompanying metadata should be deposited as well, for all categories or types of material.

## 4.2. Music Scores

**4.2.1.** Music scores, printed or in electronic format, should be subject to legal deposit.

## 4.3. Serials

**4.3.1.** Legal deposit legislation should include all types of publications issued periodically, even on an irregular basis, and loose-leaf services with updates.

**4.3.2.** Every issue of a serial should be deposited in order to build up as comprehensive a research collection as possible.

**4.3.3.** There could be exceptions to the comprehensive collecting of each issue; only the first issue of ephemeral material, such as internal newsletters of organizations, could be collected.

**4.3.4.** Serials also published in electronic format, off-line or online, should be deposited.

## 4.4. Pamphlets and Offprints

**4.4.1.** Pamphlets should be deposited, including ones with a minimum number of pages.

**4.4.2.** Offprints that are repaginated and issued for public distribution should be deposited.

**4.4.3.** Leaflets, posters, broadsides, post cards and other iconographic material could be deposited, but processing and handing procedures have to be well planned.

## 4.5. Iconographic Material

**4.5.1.** Pamphlets should be deposited, including

ones with a minimum number of pages.

### 4.6. Government Publications

**4.6.1.** Government publications should be part of any national legal deposit scheme, even if their deposit might not be compulsory for internal legal reasons.

**4.6.2.** While it might be difficult to collect all municipal and / or local government publications, administrative arrangements should be negotiated to collect them at least at a regional level.

**4.6.3.** International and intergovernmental government publications cannot be subject to national legal deposit legislation because of the jurisdictional immunity principle.

### 4.7. Maps

**4.7.1.** Maps should be part of a national legal deposit collection.

**4.7.2.** As maps can now be produced on demand by using Geographic Information System software, legal deposit of maps could become problematic. As long as the databases remain complementary to the print material, there should be no major problems.

**4.7.3.** Maps are a good example of where another national Institution, more specialized in handling the material, could get involved in the national legal deposit scheme.

### 4.8. Microforms

**4.8.1.** The microform edition of a print work should be subject to legal deposit, as is any other edition of a work.

**4.8.2.** With certain categories of material, such as newspapers, the depository could opt for the deposit of the microform edition only.

**4.8.3.** Original publications in microform format should be deposited.

### 4.9. Audio-visual Material

**4.9.1.** Sound and visual recordings, separate and combined, should be subject to legal deposit. ,All accompanying material should also be subject to deposit.

**4.9.2.** Because of the susceptibility of the carriers and equipment to technological changes and obsolescence, there could be a need to amend national copyright laws or provide the national legal deposit law with notwithstanding clauses allowing reproduction in current formats.

**4.9.3.** Networked multimedia works should also be subject to legal deposit, but all the problems related to legal deposit of electronic publications should be taken into account.

**4.9.4.** Radio and television broadcast material should be an object of legal deposit.

### 4.10. Other Types of Material

**4.10.1.** Before deciding on exactly what tpe of material should be subject to legal deposit, it is very important to evaluate the practicality of certain decisions. As an example, ephemeral material, such as internal organizational newsletters, might consume a lot of resources for a limited national historical research value.

## 5. ELECTRONIC PUBLICATIONS

**5.1.** Off-line and on-line electronic publications should be subject to legal deposit and should be deposited along with all appropriate accompanying material including proper software.

**5.2.** Dynamic on-line electronic publications (i.e. the ones kept up-to-date on an ongoing basis) should also be subject to legal deposit. The deposit could be handled through a "snapshot" deposit on a regular basis and when the title ceases to be published / produced. The first version of a dynamic on-line electronic publication should always be deposited.

**5.3.** The legislation should include provisions to ensure that registered users of the national legal deposit agency have access to the electronic material deposited.

**5.4.** To avoid abuse of the free access provided through the national legal deposit agency, access should be limited; however, publishers /producers should be required to permit a limited number of concurrent users.

**5.5.** As for audio-visual material, there may be a need to amend national copyright laws to permit the national legal deposit institution to download, and therefore reproduce, electronic publications for legal deposit purposes.

## REFERENCES:

1. ISBN Progress Repot. India. *http://www.isbn International.org/html/ progress/2001/india. html.*
2. JeanLunn. *Guidelines for Legal Deposit.* Paris, UNESCO, 1981,p.1.
3. Peter Jor Lor. *Guidelines for Legislation for National Library Services.* Paris, UNESCO, 19987. p.25.
4. A. R. Bandhyopadhyay. The Delivery of Books Act, 1954. Suggestions for a Fresh Look. *ILA Bulletin,* V36, N3, 2000. p.69-79.
5. A. R. Bandhyopadhyay. The Delivery of Books Act, 1954. Suggestions for Fresh Look. *ILA Bulletin,* V36, N3,2000. p.69-70.

6. Syed Abuzar. National Bibliographic Control and Legal Deposit in India: An overview. *In Information Management in Knowledge Society.* Kolkata, IASLIC, 2005. pp.421-422.
7. H. M. Nayak and B. R. Gopal. *Eds. South Indian Studies.* Mysore, Geetha Book House, 1990.
8. Jules LariViere. *Guidelines for Legal Deposit Legislation.* Paris, UNESCO, 2000.pp.46-53.

# 4

# Bibliographical Control in India

As stated already the enactment of Press and Registration of Books Act in 1867 sowed the seeds for some sort of bibliographic control over the publications emanating from the whole of India including South India. The purpose of the Act was to regulate and control the printing presses and later newspapers and also for the preservation of copies of books and newspapers printed in India and their registration. This is a Central Act, but the implementation was entrusted to respective State Governments. After independence, Government of India enacted Delivery of Books and Newspapers (Public Libraries) Act, 1954 to provide free delivery of books and Newspapers to the National Library, Kolkata and three designated libraries in the Country. These two acts have contributed to the genesis and emergence of legal deposit in the country and helped to achieve some sort of bibliographical control of publications emanating from the Country.

As stated in the preceding paragraph, the implementation of Press and Registration of Books Act 1867, though a Central Act was vested with the respective State Governments. As for the second Act i.e. Delivery of Books and Newspapers (Public Libraries)

1954 was concerned, it is the responsibility of the publishers concerned to conform to the provisions of the Act and deliver copies of their publications to the four designated libraries i.e. National Library, Kolkata, Central Library, Mumbai, Connemara Public Library, Chennai and Delhi Public Library, New Delhi.

After independence, in addition to the governments initiative in the form of Delivery of Books and News Papers (Public Libraries Act) 1954 for bibliographical control, initiatives have come from non-governmental organizations, learned societies and institutions such as the Library of Congress *Accession List, South Asian Bibliographer, Index India,* which are in the form of current bibliographies and retrospective bibliographies such as the *National Bibliography of Indian Literature,* 1901-1953 and *Indian Books in Print* (1967 -) though retrospective but updated annually. The launching of *Indian National Bibliography* (INB ) (1958 -) by the Central Reference Library at Calcutta is another landmark in the efforts to achieve bibliographical control in India. In addition, there were many retrospective bibliographies brought out by learned institutions and societies in the subject fields of their interest and these actions have also contributed to achieve some sort of bibliographical control of Indian publications.

## CURRENT BIBLIOGRAPHY

The foremost among the current bibliography of Indian Publications brought out by private initiative i.e. the American Libraries Book Procurement Centre, New Delhi under the title *Accessions List India,* which appeared on the scene in the year 1962. Under this programme the Library of Congress acquires publications of the world for selected libraries in the

United States. As for India was concerned *Accessions List India* was first appeared as a monthly in 1962 (Vol.1) and continued up to end of 1980 (Vol.19). In January 1981 the title was changed as *Accessions List - South Asia* (Vol.1) to publish a single consolidated list covering acquisitions from other countries in South Asia region. The last volume -16 under this title appeared in 1996 and there after ceased publication.

The *Accessions List - South Asia* was succeeded by the *South Asian Bibliographer* in 1998 under the agreement between the Library of Congress Field Office and the well known publisher Sage Publications India and the later had taken the responsibility of bringing out regularly. The *South Asian Bibliographer: A list of current publications* compiled by Library of Congress Office, New Delhi started appearing in 1998 (Vol.1) as a bimonthly in January, March, May, July, September and November and with a seventh issue in December containing author and title indexes. Each issue contains about 1000 to 1200 titles. It covers monographs, serials and audio and video recordings, maps and other materials from countries such as: Afghanistan, Bangladesh, Bhutan, Burma, Cambodia, India, Laos, Malaysia, Maldives, Mongolia, Nepal, Pakistan, Singapore, Sri Lanka and Thailand and Tibetan language publications from China, Bhutan, India, Mongolia and Nepal.

The entries are professionally prepared applying meticulously rules for cataloging and serve as Cataloging in Publications (CIP). Monographs and Serials are arranged under each country alphabetically by language and within language by main entry. The other formats are arranged in second section alphabetically by main entry by country without giving importance to language or format. Each entry contains full bibliographical details and all entries are printed in Roman script irrespective of the script of the publication. India being a largest country in South Asian region and the number of publication emanating from India are very large when compared with other countries it is but natural that the share in the acquisition programme is obviously largest. The Indian section covers languages viz: Arabic, Assamese, Bengali, English, Gujarati, Hindi, Kannada, Kashmiri, Malayalam, Marathi, Nepali, Oriya, Pali, Panjabi, Persian, Rajasthani, Sanskrit, Sindhi, Tamil, Telugu and Urdu. The entries are highly selective. Nevertheless the *South Asian Bibliographer* provides an authentic bibliographical information for publications emanating from India. It ceased publication, after five years of collaboration (1998-2002) with the last issue of Volume 5, in December 2002. It was the only printed bibliography of scholarly books devoted to the region as a whole. The reason for its discontinuation was "the increased availability of bibliographic information on South Asia over the Internet and market considerations. ..."[1]

## RETROSPECTIVE BIBLIOGRAPHIES

Retrospective bibliography lists books published in previous years as distinct from a current bibliography. These bibliographical tools also contributed to the achievement of bibliographical control of publications emanating from a particular country or region.

## NATIONAL BIBLIOGRAPHY OF INDIAN LITERATURE

Among the retrospective bibliographies mention may be made of *National Bibliography of Indian*

*Literature 1901-1953* (First series) published by Sahitya Akademi, New Delhi under the General Editorship of B. S. Kesavan. The first series of the bibliography was in four volumes covering majority of publications in Indian languages and published during the years 1962-1974. The fifth volume under the series was published in 1990 covering the period 1901-1980 including the languages: Konkani, Maithili, Manipuri, Nepali and Rajasthani. The Editor of fifth volume was K. C. Dutt.

The second series of *National Bibliography of India Literature* covering the publications in all the twenty two languages recognized by Sahitya Akademi and published during the year 1954-2000 has been launched in the year 2003 under the supervision of K. C. Dutt. The entry format, rules and regulations, guidelines, appointment of language editors, literature experts and aspects pertaining to compilation of retrospective bibliographies has been finalized. The second series is expected to cover 1.30 lakh entries against about 60,000 entries in the first series.

## INDIAN BOOKS IN PRINT

Another important retrospective bibliographical tool for English books published in India is the *Indian Books in Print* (published annually) edited by Sher Singh and Co-edited by Bhawana Singh. This is in 3 volumes. Vol.1: Author Index, Vol.2: Titles and Vol.3: Subject Guide and published by Indian Bibliographies Bureau, New Delhi. The latest is *Indian Books in Print,* 2005 in 3 volumes, 4 parts, 22nd Edition. It was first published in 1967 with a modest beginning covering the year 1952-1967. It has run into 22nd editions with the entries numbering 4,50,000 titles published till March, 2005 in India in English Language. In Volume 1: Authors, the information has been alphabetically by author and contains information about title, edition, publisher, collation, illustration and price. Vol.2: Titles arranged alphabetically by title and contains information about author, publisher, collation, illustration and price. Vol.3: Subject Guide. It consists of two parts: Part-1: Classified by Dewey Decimal Classification with feature headings and contains information about author, title, edition, publisher, collation, illustration and price. Part-2 is the Directory of Indian Publishers with full addresses.

It is a 'Complete' and 'most comprehensive' bibliographical tool for librarians, research scholars, publishers and book sellers providing access to bibliographical information of English books published in India.

## ALL INDIA INDEX TO ENGLISH BOOKS IN PRINT (AIIEBIP)

National Information Service Corporation (NISC) Hyderabad a private agency dealing with knowledge products and services, has launched the publication of world class database - *All India Index to English Books in Print* (AIIEBIP) in March, 2003 in two formats: On CD-ROM and Internet / Web-based. The main objective of this service is "to offer publicity to Indian Books in English so that information about them reaches far and wide thereby ensuring that the right book reaches the right reader at the right time". This service invites publishers both commercial and individual as well bibliographic information about their latest publications so as to achieve bibliographical control of Indian Publications and reflect the wide spectrum of Indian Publishing to the world at large. The number of records available in this database was 181, 885 + and covers 1950 and earlier to present. It is the electronic version of *Indian Books in Print*, New Delhi. AIIEBIP also includes "thousands of books not found in *Indian Books in Print*, published from India in the domain of Social Sciences, Arts, Humanities and Science and Technology". It is updated monthly on Biblio Line (Internet based service) and Quarterly on CD-ROM[2]. This online service has been withdrawn due to lack of support from Publishers, Libraries and Information Centres and individuals from March, 2008.

This is just one example of private initiative which helps to achieve some sort of bibliographical control over Indian Publications. Such type of online and CD-ROM services are very much needed for Indian language publications also so as to achieve, if not complete, near comprehensive bibliographical control of Indian Publications. Such private efforts even though brought on commercial line will go a long way in complimenting and supplementing current and retrospective bibliographical services like *Indian National Bibliography* (INB) and *Indian Books in Print* (IBP).

## BIBLIOGRAPHICAL CONTROL OF OTHER TYPES OF MATERIAL

In addition to bibliographical control of books through current and retrospective bibliographies there are variety of Indexes which help to control periodical articles, bibliographies of reference sources, guides to periodicals and serials, union catalogues to periodicals and periodicals for book reviews.

As regards Indexes to periodical literature is concerned the foremost among them are: *Index India* (1967 - ) and *Guide to Indian Periodical Literature* (1964 - ) in the field of Humanities and Social Sciences and *Indian Science Abstracts* (1965 - ) in the field of Sciences which help the academic community by citing the latest periodical literature in their respective fields. In respect of doctoral dissertations submitted to Indian Universities mention may be made of pioneering work done by Association of Indian Universities (AIU) (formerly Inter University Board of India and Ceylon) by bringing out *'Bibliography of Doctoral Dissertations accepted by Indian Universities'* for the years 1857-1970 in Humanities, Social Sciences and Sciences. This is updated by annual publications and through its current bibliography under "Theses of the Month' in its weekly journal *University News* and ICSSR's *Indian Dissertation Abstracts* (Q) (1973 - ) a quarterly publication covering Social Science dissertations is another bibliographical tool of importance. To supplement and compliment these tools on theses and dissertations several universities have been bringing out cumulative indexes of their dissertations. For example Jawaharlal Nehru University's *Dissertation Index* and *Abstracts of dissertations in Social Sciences*, 1920-1969 accepted by Aligarh Muslim University fall under this category. The compilers of bibliographies have not ignored the value and importance of reference books in the dissemination of information. A two volume *Guide to Reference Materials on India* (1974) was compiled by N. N. Gidwani and K. Navalani.

## PERIODICAL LISTS

Periodicals and serial publications play a vital role in the disseminations of nascent micro thought. In order to have control over Indian periodical and serial publications a number of tools have been published. Of many of them mention may be made of *Indian Periodicals in Print*, 2 Vols. (1973) compiled by H.N.D. Gandhi etal and *Indian Periodicals: An annotated Guide*

(Revised), compiled by N. N. Gidwani and K. Navalani. Mention also be made of important tools such as *Union Catalogue Social Science Periodicals* and *Union Catalogue of Social Science Serials* covering all States of India and brought by ICSSR, New Delhi in the 1970's and *Regional Union Catalogue of Scientific Serials* covering important cities of India and brought out by INSDOC, New Delhi in the1960's and 1970's.

## BOOK REVIEWS

Book reviews also play a very important role in drawing the attention of the scholarly and library community of current publications and their thought content and other aspects of a particular book under review. The 1970's witnessed emergence of two book reviewing periodicals viz: *Indian Book Chronicle* (FN) (1976) and *Book Review* (bimonthly) (1976-1982). In order to provide access to hundreds of book reviews appearing in the two reviewing periodicals and also in professional journals and newspapers, a new service - *Indian Book Review Index* (1975/76) was started in 1978.

## SUBJECT BIBLIOGRAPHIES

While general bibliographies such as *Indian National Bibliography* and *Indian Books in Print* provide information about all publications covering wide field of knowledge, subject bibliographies confine to specific subject field, a number of subject bibliographies covering, branches of humanities, social sciences and sciences and technologies have emerged on the Indian bibliographical scene. Of numerous subject bibliographies mention may be made of few important subject bibliographies such as: *Annotated Bibliography on the Economic History of India*, 1500-1947, Vols. 1-3; *Centre-State and Inter-State Relations in India, 1919-*

*1970: A Bibliography (1973); Indian Political Movement, 1919-1971: A systematic Bibliography (1976); Survey of Indian Agro-Economic and Allied Literature, 1947-1975: A Bibliography (1978); Writings on Indian Constitution,* 1861-1972 (1973); *Third Exhibition of Indian Scientific and Technical Books, 1966-1975: A Classified Catalogue of English titles (1976); Hindi Sahitya: Aalochana Grant-suchi, 1947-1977*

## INSTITUTIONAL CONTRIBUTION

Learned Institutions, Societies and R & D Institutions in India have also greatly contributed to the emergence of bibliographical control in India through their activities and publications. A. R. Sethi observed that "among these, the INSDOC of the CSIR and SSDC of the ICSSR are responsible, directly or indirectly, for the publication of plethora of bibliographies in various subject fields as well as material fields. By undertaking compilation, financing of projects, bulk purchase of bibliographies and other incentives they have inaugurated the era of biblio-explosion in India"[3].

There are other learned institutions and societies and academic institutions of both Central and State Governments and Private Organizations which have done considerable bibliographical work in the fields of Humanities, Social Sciences and Science ad Technology. Mention may be made of the organizations like the Indian Council of Historical Research (ICHR), Indian Council of Philosophical Research (ICPR), Indian Council of World Affairs (ICWA), Indian Council for Agriculture Research (ICAR), Indira Gandhi National Centre for Arts (IGNCA) Nehru Memorial Museum and Library, Indian Institute of Public Administration and the National Surveying agencies such as: Geological

Survey of India, Botanical Survey of India, Zoological Survey of India, Anthropological Survey of India. Archeological Survey of India, National Sahitya Akamedi, Sangeet Natak Akademi and Lalit Kala Akademi and host of other institutions have been binging out bibliographies in their fields of interest and contributing to the growth of bibliographical control of Indian Publications mostly in English Language. In addition to aforementioned learned institutions and societies, the libraries, information centre and documentation centres attached to the Central government ministries such as - Ministries of Human Resource Development, Labour, Finance, Industry, Agriculture and Tourism, Chemicals and Fertilizers have also brought out bibliographies and current awareness lists for the benefit of their user community.

The contributions of State and Central Universities in the emergence and sustenance of bibliographical control of Indian Publications is worth mentioning. The University Libraries of Banaras, Rajasthan, Delhi, Jawaharlal Nehru, Panjab, Madras, Bombay, Calcutta, Aligarh, Osmania, Andhra, Mysore, Univ. of Hyderabad, Univ. of Kerala, Bagalore, Dharwad and host of other Universities have been bringing out general and subject bibliographies and documentation lists for the benefit of their user community in particular and others in general and these efforts have greatly contributed to bibliographical control of English Publications emanating from India.

## INDIAN LANGUAGES PUBLICATIONS

The preceding paragraphs briefly deal with the bibliographical activity and control of English language publications. There is no significant bibliographical activity of Indian languages publications. The annual book production in the twenty two Indian languages listed in the eighth schedule of constitution of India is considerable and significant. Out of the total annual book production in Indian languages, the National Library received only 13,814 books in major Indian languages under DB Act, 1954 in the year 2003. This figure many not reflect the true picture of Indian languages publications. Except INB, there are no other authentic bibliographical tools which can portray the true picture of Indian languages publications. Taking in to account not so encouraging scenario of bibliographical control of Indian language publications, A. R. Sethi commented that "most of these (English) bibliographies are in English language and contain English language material alone, to the exclusion of the vast literature that is published in regional languages. In fact, the problem of bibliographical control of non-English material is more acute and urgent"[4].

The bibliographical activity in Indian languages, as it is, is very arduous and disappointing. Public initiative i.e. Central and State Government agencies and Institutions and Societies supported by Central and State Governments funds, Central and State Universities and other educational institutions both private and public and special, academic and public libraries have not shown much interest, with few exceptions, in bringing out bibliographical tools to have better picture of Indian languages publications. Sincere efforts by these institutions will go a long way to have some sort of bibliographical control over Indian languages publications. In this respect the National Library has greater responsibility in implementing the provisions DB Act, 1954 very effectively and accelerates the work of bringing out State wise language bibliographies hither to relegated to background due to known and unknown reasons.

## INDIAN NATIONAL BIBLIOGRAPHY

The enactment of Delivery of Books and News Papers (Public Libraries) Act, 1954 gave philip to the establishment of Central Reference Library (CRL) in Kolkata which was entrusted with the job of bringing out *Indian National Bibliography* (INB) to have some sort of bibliographical control of Indian Publications. According to Kochukoshy "the INB has been conceived as an authoritative bibliographical record of current Indian Publications in 14 major languages of India... received at the National Library, Kolkata under the provisions of Delivery of Books (Public Libraries) Act 1954"[5] The INB was first published as a quarterly with annual cumulations from 1958 to 1963 and it periodicity was changed to monthly in 1964.

Right from its genesis in 1958, INB could not meet the expectations of the library profession to have comprehensive and satisfactory coverage of Indian Publications. It suffers from lack of support and cooperation from the Indian Publishers to send their Publications as per the provision of DB Act, 1954 and inordinate delay between the receipt of books and the publication of INB and the erratic frequency of its publications. Dasgupta observed that "the extremely low coverage of INB, as is well known, is attributable to the total failure of the concerned authority to enforce the provisions of the Act"[6]. K.K.KochuKoshy, Librarian, Central Reference Library (CRL), Kolkata opines that "the receipt of books is poor because of the poor implementation of the Act and the same is reflected in INB also. We are trying to improve the situation. But at the same time we do not include guide books, study material, multi-volumes counted as one, duplicates not included, reprints also omitted. So there will be difference in the receipts at NL and INB"[7].

The following table provides for comparative figures of receipt of booksat the National Library, Kolkata and their inclusions in the INB.

**Table**

| *Year* | *1998-99* | *1999-2000* | *2000-2001* | *2001-2002* | *2002-2003* |
|---|---|---|---|---|---|
| National Library | 15,922 | 20,012 | 19,951 | 18,898 | 20,309 |
| INB* | 9,163 | 12,486 | 12,725 | 9,752 | 10,499 |

* *January-December each year*

**Source:** *National Library, Kolkata and Central Reference Library, Kolkata.*

From the above Table it is clear that INB includes appropriately 35 to 50% of the books received from the National Library. The National Library on its part may have excluded a number of publications from accessioning due to reasons such as ephemeral nature of publications, non-utility and lack of space for their preservation. In turn INB has set out its own criteria for non-inclusion of certain publications such as guide books, study materials, duplicates and reprints. Abuzar opines that "non-inclusion of 65% of the receipts suggests a stance of tedium to national bibliographical control program; hence no question of any effort for supplementing the data from the receipts of other three libraries arose ever. Whatever may be the reason, the coverage in the INB stands to be 15% to 20% of the total number of books produced in the Country"[8].

## LANGUAGE WISE COVERAGE OF BOOKS IN INB

The INB has been contemplated as an 'authoritative' bibliographical record of current Indian publications in 14 major languages of the Country received at the National Library, Kolkata under DB Act, 1954. The following tables present the inclusion of books of major South Indian Languages including English, Urdu, Sanskrit and Hindi in the INB for the years 1999 to 2003.

**Table**

| ↓*Language Year*→ | *1999* | *2000* | *2001* | *2002* | *2003* | *Total* |
|---|---|---|---|---|---|---|
| Telugu | 223 | 221 | 363 | 217 | 271 | 1295 |
| Kannada | 651 | 652 | 703 | 492 | 641 | 3139 |
| Tamil | 1448 | 1935 | 1312 | 670 | 981 | 6346 |
| Malayalam | 139 | 482 | 626 | 402 | 420 | 2069 |
| Urdu | 171 | 151 | 224 | 308 | 321 | 1175 |
| English | 2184 | 4001 | 3843 | 3266 | 3877 | 17171 |
| Hindi | 1243 | 1116 | 1732 | 1535 | 1425 | 7071 |
| Sanskrit | NA | NA | NA | NA | NA | — |

*Source: Central Reference Library, Kolkata*

It is evident from the above Table that the coverage of Telugu Publications in the INB is not encouraging when compared with the other three South Indian Languages viz. Tamil, Kannada and Malayalam. This is due to poor receipt of only 500 to 600 Telugu books at the National Library annually under DB Act, 1954. The following Table provides an idea as to the receipt of number of publications in major South Indian Languages including English, Hindi and Sanskrit at the National Library Kolkata under DB Act, 1954 for five year period.

**Table**

| ↓Language Year → | 1998-99 | 1998-2000 | 2000-2001 | 2001-2002 | 2002-2003 | Total |
|---|---|---|---|---|---|---|
| Teugu | 576 | 484 | 452 | 360 | 365 | 2237 |
| Kannada | 793 | 966 | 656 | 590 | 683 | 3688 |
| Tamil | 1929 | 2620 | 2903 | 2823 | 2966 | 13241 |
| Malayalam | 368 | 860 | 603 | 310 | 401 | 2542 |
| Urdu | 217 | 245 | 201 | 311 | 357 | 1331 |
| English | 4529 | 5471 | 6734 | 7309 | 6625 | 30668 |
| Hindi | 1591 | 1514 | 2043 | 2280 | 2272 | 9700 |
| Sanskrit | 106 | 74 | 99 | 138 | 145 | 562 |

*Source: National Library, Kolkata*

As stated already INB includes about 30% to 50% books received at the National Library. With exception to Tamil, the receipt of books in Telugu, Kannada and Malayalam at the National Library and their inclusion in the INB is not encouraging. It appears that the response to provisions of DB Act from the publishers in Andhra Pradesh, Karnataka and Kerala is not satisfactory.

## LANGUAGE BIBLIOGRAPHIES OF INB

The scope and price of Roman script issues of INB made it difficult for private individuals and smaller organizations like district and town public libraries, school and college libraries and libraries under private / voluntary organizations in the country to subscribe to INB. It was felt that the local needs and the needs of individual linguistic States can be met by bringing out separate annual bibliographies of books in Indian languages in the script of respective languages. The language bibliographies will go a long way in meeting the requirements small and medium size public and academic libraries, private individuals and smaller organizations. It was also felt "that the publication of the language bibliographies would contribute indirectly to the development of the regional languages and also fulfill the long felt need to reference books like bibliographies in regional languages"[9].

The language bibliographies help to achieve State level bibliographical control of language publications emanating from the States of the Country. As for South India is concerned the language bibliographies of Telugu, Tamil, Kannada and Malayalam will go a long way to help achieve regional bibliographical control of publications of major South Indian languages emanating from South India. In 1959 the then Ministry of Scientific and Cultural Affairs, Government of India in cooperation with respective State governments initiated action of printing and publication of language bibliographies. The following **Table** provides information about the publication of language bibliographies in the four South Indian languages - Telugu, Tamil, Kannada and Malayalam.

| *Language* | *Publisher* | *Volumes Published* | *Total* |
|---|---|---|---|
| Telugu | Govt. of A.P. | 1958-1974, 1980-83 | 20 |
| Tamil* | Govt. of Tamilnadu | 1958-1974, '1984-86, 1987-88 (CRL) | 22 |
| Kannada | Govt. of Karnataka | 1958-72, 1981-92, 2004, 2005 (In CD Form) | 29 |
| Malayalam | Govt. of Kerala | 1958-89 (including two 10-year cumulation: 1971-80 and 1981-1990) | 31 |

*Source: Central Reference Library Brochure, 1992*

* *According to information received from the Librarian, Connemara Public Library, Chennai Printed Annual Volumes were brought out for the years 1958-1981 i.e. 24 volumes. For the years 1982-2005 the entries for the annual volumes are in MSSform and they are yet to be printed.*

## LANGUAGE BIBLIOGRAPHIES IN OTHER LANGUAGES

In addition to language bibliographies so far brought out in Telugu, Tamil, Kannada and Malayalam, as shown in the preceeding Table, the following Table provides details of language bibliographies brought out in other languages such as Assamese, Bengali, Gujarati, Hindi, Marathi, Oriya, Panjabi, Sanskrit and Urdu.

**Table**

| *Language* | *Publisher* | *Volume Published* | *Total Number* |
|---|---|---|---|
| Assamese | State Central Library | 1959, 60, 61, 1962-70 (CRL) | 11 |
| Bengali | Govt. of West Bengal | 1958-March 1965, 1979-81 (CRL) | 11 |
| Gujarati | Govt. of Gujarat | 1958-61, 1962-71 | 14 |
| Hindi | Govt. of Uttar Pradesh | 1958-88, 1989 | 31 |
| Marathi | Govt.of Maharashtra | 1958-70 | 12 |
| Oriya | Orissa Sahitya Academi | 1958-63, 1979-80 (CRL) | 08 |
| Punjabi | Govt. of Panjab | 1958-62, 1971-74 | 09 |
| Sanskrit | Central Reference Library (CRL) | 1958-62, 1963-67, 1968-1977 | 20 |
| Urdu | Govt. of Uttar Pradesh | 1958-65, 1961-62, 1983-85, 1986-87, 1988-1990 | 18 |

***Source:*** *Central Reference Library, Kolkata, Brochure, 1992.*

The purpose of bringing out language bibliographies is to develop the regional languages of the Country and fulfill the long felt need to reference books like bibliographies in regional languages. Due to administrative and other problems some of the language bibliographies were behind the schedule. Therefore Central Reference Library came forward for publishing some of the language bibliographies like Assamese, Bengali, Oriya, Sanskrit and Tamil.

## MODERNIZATION OF INB

Before 2000 the compilation and generation of INB was mostly dependent on manual operations. In order to make it more useful and effective bibliographical tool and to reduced delay in its production the processes of compilation and generation was 'fully automated' since June 2000. For the generation of INB customized version of Libsys 4.0 software is being used. Since June 2000 all the monthly issues of INB have been published regularly. In addition to automation of the process of compilation and publication of INB retro conversion of INB records was taken up. The records of INB since its inception in 1958 - had been converted into electronic data. It has been stated that almost six lakhs bibliographical records belonging to different Indian languages is available now with Central Reference Library (CRL). Efforts are being made to make the data available online[10].

## REFERENCES


1. *http://www.loc.gov/acq/ouop/delhi/newssab.html*
2. *www.nisc.com*
3. A. R. Sethi. Bibliographical Control of Indian Publications in English: An Assessment. *ILABulletin*, V.18, No. 1-2April-September, 1982. p.17.
4. A. R. Sethi. Bibliographical Control of Indian Publication in English: An Assessment. *ILABulletin, V.18, No. 122, 1982. p.14.*
5. K. K. Kochukoshy. The Indian National Bibliography Service its inception in 1958. *In National Bibliographical Control: Problems and Perspectives.* Ed. by A. A. N. Raju and L. S.

Ramaiah, New Delhi, Allied, 2003. p.94.

6. A. K. Dasgupta. What ails the INB? *In National Bibliographical Control: Problems and Perspectives.* Ed. by A. A. N. Raju and L. S. Ramaiah. New Delhi, Allied, 2003. p.349.
7. K. K. Kochukoshy. Communication dated 02.05.2006 to Prof. A. A. N. Raju.
8. Syed Abuzar. National Bibliographic Control and Legal Deposit in India: An overview. *In Information Management in Knowledge Society,* Kolkata, IASLIC,2005.p.426.
9. The Indian National Bibliography 1958-1992. *Brochure.* Kolkata, Central Reference Library, 1992. p.2.
10. *http://www.crlindia.gov.in/retro.htm*

# 5

# Working of the Press and Registration of Books Act, 1867 (PRB Act, 1867) in The States of India

## BACKGROUND

As stated in the preceding Chapter-3, legal deposit ensures one or more libraries in the Country or constituent States to get free copies of newly printed books / documents / periodicals and newspapers from the printers / publishers in the Country. The origin of legal deposit in the world goes back to 16th Century when King Francis-I of France established a legal depository in 1537 for the printed materials including the laws and parliamentary debates of that Country. The King wanted to collect and gather the current and the future production of all editions of books which deserved to be seen in order to ensure that "it would be always possible to refer to the original works as first published and not modified[1] The idea of legal deposit got momentum and all the progressive governments of the World initiated actions to have legal deposit laws in their respective countries. U.K. took the lead in 1662 followed by U.S.A. in 1790. The main purpose behind legal deposit enactment was to preserve the nation's documentary heritage to the future generations. According to Meshram the four features contributing to the success of legal deposit acts are:

1. *Exhaustiveness of the material received.*
2. *Its proper preservation.*
3. *Regular information about its availability in the designated libraries through lists and bibliographies; and*
4. *Free and direct access to the material so collected[2].*

To meet the information requirements of British and European Scholars, the Office bearers of the Royal Asiatic Society of Great Britain and Ireland mooted the idea of collecting, maintaining and preserving books published in colonial India at the India Office Library in London. The idea was conveyed to the Secretary of State for India in May 1863. This prompted authorities to bring out Press and Registration of Books Act in 1867 to have one copy of every publication in India and another copy in England. The specific reason for bringing out this act was to oversee and maintain law and order situation in the colonial India after the first war of Independence in 1857 and to make available every book printed in India for the use of Scholars in England. After India attained independence in 1947 the practice of sending copies of each publication as per the provisions of Act was suspended.

The Act, which was passed in the year 1867 by the British Colonial Rulers, was to regulate and control the printing presses and later newspapers and also for the preservation of copies of books and newspapers printed in India and their registration. The positive aspect of this Act was to preserve the intellectual output of the country for posterity. The negative aspect of the Act was to keep an eye on the intellectual awakening in the country, which may go against the interests of the colonial rulers. The Preamble of the Act states that "an Act for the regulation of printing presses and newspapers, for preservation of copies of books and newspapers published in India and for the registration of such books and newspapers".

## OBJECTIVES

The main objectives of act are to: *1. Secure information from printing houses or establishments and their publications, 2. Preserve copies of every book and newspaper printed in India, 3. Regulate Printing Presses and Newspapers and 4. Prevent publication of anonymous literature.*

## PROVISIONS OF THE ACT

The Act contains seven parts as mentioned below:

1. Part-I Preliminary (Sections 1 and 2)
2. Part-II Of Printing Presses and Newspapers (Sections 3 to 8C)
3. Part-III Delivery of Books (Sections 9 to 11B)
4. Part-IV Penalties (Sections 12 to 17)
5. Part-V Registration of Books (Sections 18 and 19)

6. Part-V-A Registration of Newspapers (Sections 19A to 19L)
7. Part/VI Miscellaneous (Sections 20 - 23)

## IMPORTANT PROVISIONS

The seven Parts of the Act consist forty-six sections covering various provisions of the Act. Some of the important provisions are briefly presented below:

## DELIVERY OF PRINTED BOOKS AND NEWSPAPERS

Section 9 (Part-III) of the Act deals with the delivery of printed books as gratis to the government. This section stipulates that printed copies of the whole of every book which shall be printed in India together with all maps and prints, etc, be delivered by the Printer at such place and to such officer as the State Government shall by notification in the official gazette from time to time. The Printer has to deliver *three copies* of each publication free of expense to the State Government within a calendar year.

Likewise Section 11A (Part-III) of the Act stipulates that the Printer of every newspaper shall deliver at such place and to such officer as the State Government by notification in the official gazette, direct, and free of expense to the government, *two copies* of each issue of such newspaper as soon as it is published.

## PENALTIES FOR NOT DELIVERING BOOKS AND NEWSPAPERS

Section 16 (Part-IV) of the act stipulates that if any printer of any book fails to deliver three copies of the book printed by him, he shall be fined not exceeding Rs.50/- (Rupees fifty) for each default by a Magistrate having jurisdiction in the place where the book was printed.

Likewise section 16-A (Part-IV) stipulates that if any printer of any newspaper published in India neglects to deliver the copies of the same, shall be punishable on conviction by a Magistrate having jurisdiction in the place where the newspaper is printed with a fine which may extend to Rs.50/- (Rupees fifty) for every default. These two provisions i.e. 16 and 16A are analogous to Sections 3 and 3A of Delivery of Books and Newspapers (Public Libraries) Act, 1954.

## REGISTRATION OF BOOKS AND NEWSPAPERS

Section 18 (Part-V) of the Act stipulates that such officer shall keep at such office and books so received as the State Government shall appoint for this purpose. The said officer has to maintain a catalogue of books printed in India wherein shall register a memorandum of each and every book received by it. The memorandum contains fourteen particulars. These included full bibliographical details of each book and in addition consist whether the book is printed or lithographed, the name and residence of the proprietor of the copyright or of any portion of such copyright.

Section 19A(Part-VA) of the Act stipulates that a catalogue of registers of books shall be published at the end of each quarter in the official gazette and copy of the same has to be sent to the Central Government.

Section 19 B (Part-VA) of the Act states that the Press Registrar shall maintain in the prescribed manner a register of newspapers. The said register shall contain full details of every newspaper published in India. These details include: title, language, periodicity, name of the editor, printer, publisher, place of printing, average number of pages, average number of copies printed, retail selling price and names and addresses of owners of the newspaper. Section 19 G of (Part-VA) of the Act stipulates that the Press Registrar shall prepare an annual report containing summary of the information obtained by him during the previous year in respect of newspapers in India and giving an account of working of such newspapers and copies thereof shall be forwarded to the Central Government.

It may be pointed that this Act is a Central Act but implementation of provisions of the Act has been entrusted to the State Governments. As per the provisions of the Act only the printer is held responsible while the publisher is not touched.

## WORKING OF THE ACT IN THE STATES OF INDIA:

This is a Central Act and Certain Provisions were left to the concerned States for implementation. The Central Government has made the Registrar of Newspapers (Central) Rules 1956 and assigned their implementation to the Registrar of Newspapers for India, New Delhi. The respective State Governments have also made their statutory rules for its implementation. Under the PRB Act, 1867 all the State Governments are expected to acquire and send copies of all books printed anywhere in India, free of cost, to Parliament Library[3]. The following paragraphs briefly deal with the working of the Act in various States of India.

**MAHARASTHRA:** In Maharasthra, the Examiner of books and Publications, Maharasthra State, Mumbai is the notified Officer. The State Central Library, Town Hall, Mumbai and Divisional Libraries at Nagpur and Pune are notified libraries for the receipt of publications as per the provisions of the Act.

As per the executive order of the Govt. of Maharasthra, a copy of every book printed in the State is procured by the Examiners and forwarded to the Parliament Library, New Delhi. Every printer in the State has to send one copy under clause (a) and the second copy under clause (b) of section 9 of the Act of every book printed in the State of Maharasthra. The designated agency is the Examiner of Books who receives copies of books from the Printers.

As per the statutory Rules formulated by the Government of Maharasthra, the receipt of books by the designated agency is as follows:

1. The Examiner of Books and Publications, Maharashtra State, Mumbai:
   *Two copies of every book.*
2. State Central Library, Mumbai
   *One copy of every book.*
3. The Government Divisional Library, Pune:
   *One copy of every book.*
4. The Government Divisional Library, Nagpur:
   *One copy of every book.*

Thus a printer has to send a total five copies of every printed book to the designated agencies in Maharashtra. The Examiner of Books and Publications, Mumbai receives two copies of every newspaper including every edition there of which is not a mere reprint. The Director of Libraries, Maharashtra State Mumbai receives one copy of every newspaper.

The Examiner of Books and Publications prepares quarterly catalogue of receipt of books for publication in the Official Gazette of Maharashtra. After the preparation of quarterly catalogues books received under section 9(a) of the Act are disposed of by the Examiner of Books and Publications as outlined above. According to Meshram the Record Office Mumbai handed over a total number of 30,000 books received under PRB Act, 1867 to the Central Library, Mumbai in 1947. At present the total number of books and periodicals received under the provisions of the Act by the State Central Library was 2,50,000. Every year the State Bibliography is prepared by the State Central Library. As the Penal provisions in the Act are not stringent, about 25% of books and periodicals printed and published in the State are not received in the depository libraries[4].

**GUJARAT:** As per the provisions of PRB Act, 1867 and the Statutory Rules framed by the Govt. of Gujarat the following designated libraries receive copies of books printed in the State:

1. Copyright Section, Gujarat Vidyapith Library, Ahmedabad. *One Copy*
2. Copyright Section, State Central Library, Granthalaya Bhavan, Gandhinagar. *Two Copies*
3. Copyright Section, Central Library, Baroda. *One Copy*
4. Commissionerate of Information, Sachivalaya Central Library, Gandhinagar. *One copy*

The receipt of books language wise as per the provisions of the Act by the copyright Section, State Central Library for a period of five years i.e. 1998-99 to 2002-03 was as follows:

| *Year* | | *Language* | | *Total* |
|---|---|---|---|---|
| | *Gujarati* | *English* | *Hindi* | |
| 1998-1999 | 445 | 92 | NIL | 537 |
| 1999-2000 | 900 | 67 | 18 | 985 |
| 2000-2001 | 2732 | 169 | 140 | 3041 |
| 2001-2002 | 1415 | 51 | 20 | 1486 |
| 2002-2003 | 1251 | 105 | 52 | 1408 |
| Total: | 6743 | 484 | 230 | 7457 |

***Note:*** *The above figures do not include text books of schools, colleges, etc.*

From the above Table one can infer that the total receipt of books by the designated libraries in Gujarat is not encouraging. During the five year period the State Government has received only 7457 books covering the languages such as Gujarati, English and Hindi. Out of the five year total receipts in Gujarati language, the State language, occupies the prime position - the total receipts being 6743 books followed by English 484 and Hindi 230 books. Perhaps these figures do not reflect the actual printing and publishing scenario in Gujarat State.

**ORISSA :** As per Section 20 of the Press and Registration of Books Act, 1867, and the rules framed by Government of Orissa, Harekrishna Mehtab State Central Library, Bhubaneshwar, receives two copies of each and every publication from the printers of the State. The third copy is received by the Sahitya Akademi, Bhubaneshwar. Of the two copies received by the State Central Library, one copy is kept in the Depository Section and the Second copy is sent to the circulation section. The following Table provides figures of the receipt of books during the years 1998-99 to 2002-03.

**Table**

| *Year* | *No. of Titles received* |
|---|---|
| 1998-1999 | 1888 |
| 1999-2000 | 1184 |
| 2000-2001 | 1441 |
| 2001-2002 | 1705 |
| 2002-2003 | 1738 |

**RAJASTHAN :** The PRB Act, 1867 was not so far implemented in Rajasthan. Draft Public Library Bill was prepared for implementation. In the said draft library bill, as per the section 20 of PRB Act, 1867, rules were framed and in the said draft rules it was suggested that every printer in the State has to submit one copy of the printed book to Radhakrishnan State Central Library, Jaipur.

**UTTAR PRADESH :** In Uttar Pradesh also the working of the PRB Act, 1867 is very discouraging. According to brief note received from Prof. N. R. Satyanarayana, the registration of Newspapers and Journals is done at the Office of the District Magistrate of each district. For example in Lucknow District whatever is published is submitted to office of the District Magistrate. The deposited material is shifted to the District Information Officer at the Information and Public Relations Office at the District Office. The data pertaining to the registered material at the District Office is compiled and later the data is submitted to the State Information Officer at the State Headquarters i.e. Lucknow. The State Office is called "Information and Public Relations Directorate" (Soachana evam Jansampark Nideshalay) at Lucknow. This Office is supposed to receive data from all the District Information Officers (Zilla Soachana Adikari). It appears that the District Information Officers does not provide any data on the receipts as they give less priority in gathering data on the receipt of periodical publications. Most of the periodicals received for registration are not properly maintained and they disappear after couple of months. Therefore, it is rather difficult to get reliable data on the receipt of journals at the District Information Offices in the State[5]. The following Table provides detail position of Newspapers and Periodicals published in Lucknow District in 2007.

The above information is only about Lucknow District. The information about the registration of Books, Newspapers and Journals in other districts of

**Table**

| *Sl. No.* | *Language:* | *Daily* | *Weekly* | *Bimonthly* | *Monthly* | *Qtly* | *Half yearly* | *Annual* | *Total* |
|---|---|---|---|---|---|---|---|---|---|
| 1 | Urdu | 21 | 36 | 05 | 08 | — | — | — | 70 |
| 2 | Hindi | 48 | 297 | 46 | 36 | 16 | 01 | 01 | 445 |
| 3 | English | 04 | 02 | 01 | — | — | — | — | -7 |
| | Total: | 73 | 335 | 52 | 44 | 16 | 01 | 01 | 522 |

Uttar Pradesh is not available. As regards printed books no data is available even from Lucknow District. It appears that the working of PRB Act, 1867 in Uttar Pradesh is very disappointing.

**WEST BENGAL :** According to the provisions of PRB Act, 1867, the Printer is supposed to submit three (3) copies of a book printed. But now a days Publishers and even authors send the books. The Act remained practically defunct for a long time after independence. In recent years, as books are selected for library purchase and forwarding recommendations to the RRRLF, publishers and authors rather than Printers are taking interest in sending the books. Printers are either unaware or oblivious or uninterested in submitting books.

Of the three copies received one copy is sent to the Parliament Library in Delhi, one copy is sent to the State Central Library, West Bengal, one copy is retained in the PRB office for preparing a record assigning a unique registration number to each book, preparation of descriptive catalogue, and a synopsis of the book. After the official paraphernalia is over, the book is gifted to a Public Library on first come first serve basis.

It is difficult to tell exactly how many printers fail to submit books or what the percentage of books received is. But a large number, mostly from non-urban areas and small publishers and printers remain un-submitted.

The fine for defaulters is Rs.50/- (Rupees fifty) only per book, prices of books are much more these days. Printers / publishers in Kolkata metropolitan area can send books by messengers but printers / publishers of other areas have to spend a good sum of money as postage charge. The PRB office cannot do much as court cases are expensive, time consuming and dependent on manpower.

The office lacks suitable and adequate number of staff. Work had been pending for a long time. The Printed Catalogue has not been prepared for books received in the last ten (10) years. It is being planned to complete this pending work in next six (6) months.

Much of printing work was pending with the Bengal Government Press. Paucity of staff is a major hindrance according to officers at the PRB Office. But the single most important factor is lack of awareness among the general public and the printers. Some printers and publishers think that after the advent of IT in printing, the Act is now not relevant. The office cannot tell of any programme of generating awareness[6].

**Table : Number of books (titles) received per year by the Office of the Registrar of Publications, Govt. of West Bengal**

| *Language:* | *1998-99* | *1999-00* | *2000-01* | *2001-02* | *2002-03* |
|---|---|---|---|---|---|
| Bengali | 1504 | 1553 | 2721 | | 2897 |
| English | 55 | 62 | 161 | | 190 |
| Hindi | 2 | 3 | 1 | | 9 |
| Sanskrit | — | — | — | | — |
| Urdu | 1 | 5 | — | | 33 |
| Nepali | — | 8 | 6 | | — |
| Santali | — | — | 3 | | — |
| Other | — | 1 Arabic | — | | — |

**NORTH EASTERN STATES :** The North Eastern States of India comprise of Arunachal Pradesh, Assam, Manipur, Meghalaya, Tripura, Nagaland, Mizoram and Sikkim. Only in two States i.e. Manipur and Mizoram Public Library Legislation has been enacted. In Assam efforts are being made for the enactment of public library legislation and the draft bill for this purpose was prepared and submitted to the Government of Assam for consideration.

Not much information is available on the state of working of Press and Registration of Books Act, 1867 in North East Indian. In the draft library bill pending with the Govt. of Assam it is proposed under Chapter-13 'Press and Registration of Books Act' certain amendments to the PRB Act, 1867[7].

As per the suggested amendments every printer in the State has to submit two copies and the two copies will be distributed to: 1. State Central Library-cum-Information Centre, Guwahati and 2. District Library from where the book is published. The Director of Public Libraries is the Registrar of Books and also Ex-Officio Head of State Bibliographic and Documentation Section. The District Librarians of respective districts are made ex-officio Registrars of Books of the Districts and are responsible for the collection of books published in the Districts concerned. The District Librarian is expected to keep one copy of each of the book in the District Library and should be preserved carefully and made available for reference and research purposes.

## TARDY IMPLEMENTATION OF THE ACT

The foregoing account of the working of the Act in various States of India indicates that the Act was not vigorously implemented except in the Southern States of India. Some of the State governments have not given any importance to implement the provisions of the Act and help in the realization of bibliographical control of Indian Publications. This particular aspect has not been given any importance in the scheme of

State Governments developmental plans and schemes.

R. Rama Swamy has made a study in the year 1998, of receipt of books as per the provisions of Act by the State Central Libraries in the Country. The study covered 27 States and Union Territories and concluded that only seven State Central Libraries in the States of Andhra Pradesh, Goa, Gujarat, Karnataka, Maharashtra, Orissa and West Bengal have been receiving copies of printed books from the printers of respective States. The total number of books received annually under this Act till the end of 1988 is as follows[8].

**Table**

| *S.No.* | *Name of the State* | *No. of books received annually* | *Total Number of Books Received* |
|---|---|---|---|
| 1 | Andhra Pradesh | 1,200 | 47,720 |
| 2 | Goa | 66 | — |
| 3 | Gujarat | 1,315 | 28,240 |
| 4 | Karnataka | 14,408 | 87,315 |
| 5 | Maharasthra | 12,000 | 2,23,856 |
| 6 | Orissa | 300 | 3,000 |
| 7 | West Bengal | 2000 | 25,000 |

## WORKING OF THE ACT IN ANDHRA PRADESH

Andhra Pradesh is one of the leading States of Indian Union where a system of Public Libraries are functioning at different levels in the State right from the State Central Library as an apex library down to the village libraries and Book Deposit Centres. The system is a result of A. P. Public Libraries Act of 1960, which provides for a separate department of public libraries with Director of Public Libraries as its administrative head.

As per section 20 (Part-VI) of the Act, Govt. of Andhra Pradesh have framed rules (Andhra Pradesh Press and Registration of Books Rules, 1960) vide GO Ms. No. 2104, Home (General-A) Department dated 10.10.1960 (See Annexure-1). In GO Ms No.235 Home (General-A) Department dated 11.02.1976, Govt. of A. P., have changed the designation of "Registrar of Books" as "Registrar of Publications". In GO Ms. No. 286 Education, dated 27.03.1973, Govt. of A. P. directed that the Director of Public Libraries (DPL) shall be Ex-Officio Registrar of Publications so as to ensure proper implementation of the provisions of Act in the entire State of A.P. With the help of District Magistrates and the Commissioner of Police Hyderabad City, the Registrar of Publications is implementing the sections 9 (delivery of gratis copies), 10 (receipt of copies), 11 (disposal of copies), 11A (Copies of newspapers), 18 (registration of memoranda of books) and 19 (Publication of memoranda registered) i.e. the functions relating to "delivery of books" and registration of books".

Sections 3, 4, 5, 7, 8, 8-A, 8-B, 8-C, 12, 13, 14, 15, 15-A, 16, 16-A, 16-B and 17 are dealt with by the District Magistrates / Commissioners of Police. These sections deal with "starting of printing presses and newspapers" and "penalties".

## RECEIPT OF PUBLICATIONS BY THE OFFICE OF THE REGISTRAR OF PUBLICATIONS

As per section 9 (Part-III) of the Act and as per the A. P. Press and Registration of Books Rules, 1960 framed by the Govt. of A. P., the Office of the Registrar of Publications receives *three copies* of every book printed within the state of A. P. (Rules 4 and 5). Similarly as per section 11-A (Part-III) of the Act, the Office of the Registrar of Publications receives *two copies* of each issue of such newspaper. Out of three copies of all books received, one copy is deposited in the 'Reference Library' maintained by the Office of the Registrar of Publications, the second copy is deposited at State Central Library (SCL), Hyderabad and the remaining third copy is sent to Parliament Library, New Delhi. The two copies of each issue of newspaper(s) received at the Registrar's Office are preserved only for two years.

As per Section 19 (Part-V) of the Act and as per the rules framed by Govt. of A. P. quarterly catalogues prepared on the basis of the receipt of books at the Office of the Registrar of Publications, should be published in the official gazette for the information of the public. But this is not being done due to administrative constraints.

## CONSTRAINTS IN THE EFFECTIVE IMPLEMENTATION OF THE ACT

The Registrar of Publications, Govt. of A. P. has been facing some problems in the effective implementation of certain provisions of the Act and Rules framed by the Govt. of A. P. Rule 7 (a) states that "every keeper of printing press shall within *ten days* of the first day of January, the first day of April, the first day of July and the first day of October each year forward to the concerned District Magistrate or if the Press is situated within the limits of twin cities of Hyderabad and Secunderabad, to the Commissioner of Police, Hyderabad a return in the 'format'.... of all the books printed at his press in the quarter immediately preceding the said dates, or if no books have been published at the Press, a statement to that effect".

The Rule 7 (b) states that "The Commissioner of

Police and the District Magistrate shall send to the Registrar within 26 days after the close of each quarter, a consolidated quarterly return in Form-II.... all the books printed and issued from various printing processes within their respective jurisdictions during the quarter". This provision is not satisfactorily implemented.

The concerned District Magistrate / Commissioner of Police are not able to initiate proper action to get quarterly reports from the printing presses due to their pre-occupation with other important and pressing government business. In the present day where the Government is pre-occupied with developmental activities, getting quarterly reports from the printing presses gets least priority in the scheme of things of the government. The result is that the Registrar of Publications is not able to get quarterly list of publications to initiate action to get such of those publications from the printers as per the provisions of Act and Rules. The provisions of the Act is not implemented effectively mostly at the district level. The situation is somewhat better in Hyderabad Police Commissionerate, where sixty per cent (60%) of printing presses have been conforming to the provisions of the Act.

## NEED FOR COOPERATION AND COORDINATION

For effective implementation of the Act, the cooperation and coordination of the Government Departments such as Home Department, Commercial Taxes, Municipal Administration, Panchayat Raj and the District Collectorates is very essential. The declaration submitted at the time of starting a new printing press to the District Magistrate / Commissioner of Police has to be regularly communicated to the Registrar of Publications so as to enable him to know the state of printing activity in the State and initiate necessary administrative measures to get the printed books, periodicals and newspapers from such printing presses.

## NUMBER OF BOOKS RECEIVED

It has been estimated that since 1953 the Registrar of Publications has received over 50,000 books and these are maintained as Reference Collections. The Table (See Annexure-2) provides an idea of the number of printing presses at work in Andhra Pradesh and the number of newspapers, periodicals and books registered at the Office of the Registrar of Publications, Govt. of A. P., between the years 1998-99 and 2003-04.

The Office of the Registrar of Publications is maintaining a catalogue of these publications and the quarterly lists have to be published in the official gazette as per the provisions of the Act and Rules. This is not being done at present due to administrative difficulties such as lack of sufficient staff and infrastructure.

## BOOK PURCHASE UNDER RRRLF SCHEME

The Rajah Ram Mohan Roy Library Foundation (RRRLF), Kolkata provides matching grant for the purchase of books every year to the respective State Governments. The Department of Public Libraries, Govt. of A. P. through Press Notification invites specimen copies of books from Publishers and Authors with the condition that "as per the Publication Act, in respect of books printed in Andhra Pradesh, 03 copies must be submitted to the Registrar of Publications...they should submit the Xerox copy of the acknowledgement from the Registrar of Publications, Hyderabad or any other evidence to the effect that they have submitted 3 copies to the Registrar of Publications".

This condition insist the Publishers / Authors to submit three copies of each publication to the Registrar of Publications if they wish to consider their publications for purchase under the said scheme along with one more copy for the said purpose. This condition indirectly compels the Publishers / Authors to conform to the provisions of the Act and the receipt of publications for registration at the Office of the Registrar of Publications, Govt. of A. P., is some what encouraging.

Andhra Pradesh is one of the few states in the Country to have a separate Office of the Registrar of Publications to take charge of printed books and other publications received under the provisions of the Act. The Act is working satisfactorily though not vigorously due to administrative constraints and lack of support and cooperation from the implementing agencies. It appears that the working of the Act is far better in Andhra Pradesh than most of the States of the Indian Union.

Annexure-I:

## GOVERNMENT OF ANDHRA PRADESH

**[G.O. Ms. No. 2104, Home (General-A) Department, dated 10th October, 1960]**

**[G.O. Ms. No. 235, Home (General-A) Department, Dated 11th February, 1976]**

ABSTRACT

RULES - Press and Registration of Books Act, 1867— Rules under Section 20 - Integration of Andhra and Hyderabad Rules - Integrated Rules - Published.

---

*ORDER:-*

The following notification will be published in the *Andhra Pradesh Gazette.* -

NOTIFICATION

In exercise of the powers conferred by Section 20 of the Press and Registration of Books Act, 1867 (Central Act 25 of 1867) and in super session of all the previous rules on the subject, the Governor of Andhra Pradesh hereby makes the following rules.

RULES

1. In these rules, unless the context otherwise requires:-
2. In these rules, unless the context otherwise requires:-
   (a) 'Registrar' means the Registrar of Publications, Andhra Pradesh;
   (b) 'The Act' means the Press and Registration of Books Act, 1867 (Central Act 25 of 1867);
   (c) 'Section' means a section of the Act.
3. For the purpose of Section 5(2) no person shall be recognized as an agent of a printer or a publisher unless he holds a duly executed power

of attorney authorizing him to appear before a competent Magistrate and to make and to subscribe the requisite declaration on behalf of such printer or publisher.

4. Three copies of every book printed within the State of Andhra Pradesh shall, as required by or under Section 9, be delivered to the Registrar at his office.

5. Out of the three copies of all the books delivered under Section 9 of the Act, the Registrar shall deposit one copy in a separate library which shall be constituted a reference library and forward with reference to Section 11 of the Act, one copy to the State Central Library, Hyderabad referred to in clause(a) of Section 8 of the Andhra Pradesh Public Libraries Act, 1960, and the remaining copy to the Parliament Library, Parliament House, New Delhi.

6. The receipt referred to in Section 10 of the Act shall be in the following form:-

"I, A. B., Registrar of Publications, Andhra Pradesh, do hereby acknowledge to have received from C.D., Printer..............................................

copy/copies of ..................................................

..............with a Memorandum of the particulars specified in the rules made under Section 20 of the Press and Registration of Books Act, 1867 (Central Act 25 of 1867).

7. (a) Every keeper of a printing press shall within ten days of the first day of January, the first day of April, the first day of July and the first day of October, of each year, forward to the concerned District Magistrate or if the Press is situated within the limits of the twin cities

of Hyderabad and Secunderabad to the Commissioner of Police, Hyderabad, a return in Form-1 appended to these rules, of all the books printed at his Press in the quarter immediately proceeding the said dates, or if no books have been printed at his Press, a statement to that effect.

(b) The Commissioner of Police and the District Magistrate shall send to the Registrar within 20 days after the close of each quarter, a consolidated quarterly return in Form-II appended to these rules of all the books printed at and issued from the various printing process within their respective jurisdictions during that quarter.

8. The Catalogue of books printed within the State of Andhra Pradesh and referred to in Section 18 of the Act shall be kept by the Registrar at his office.

9. The Registrar shall forward to the Secretary to the Government of Andhra Pradesh in the Home Department at the end of each quarter an extract from the catalogue of the books registered during the quarter. Similar extracts shall be forwarded quarterly to each District Magistrate and the Commissioner of Police in respect of the books printed within their jurisdictions.

10. Every book or paper other than a newspaper, shall have printed on it the particulars mentioned in Section 3 with full names and addresses of the author, printer, publisher, editor and keeper of the press, and the date on which the book or the paper other than a newspaper, was delivered out of press.

11. At the time of delivery of the copies of the books under rule 4 the printer shall furnish the Registrar with a memorandum containing the following particulars, duly dated and signed by he printer and countersigned by the publisher both of whom shall subscribe to a declaration in the form specified below vouching for the correctness of the particulars furnished by them:

(1) The title of the book and the contents of the title page with translation into English such title and contents when it is not in the English language;

(2) The language in which the book is written;

(3) The name of (a) the author (b) the translator, and (c) the editor of the book or any part thereof:

(4) The subject matter of the book;

(5) (a) The place of printing, and (b) The place of publication;

(6) (a) The name of firm of the printer, and (b) The name of firm of the publisher;

(7) The date of delivery from the Press and of the publication;

(8) The number of sheets, leaves or pages in the book;

(9) The size of the book;

(10) The number of the edition;

(11) The number of copies of which the edition consists;

(12) Whether the book sis printed or cyclostyled or lithographed;

(13) The price at which the book is sold to the public;

(14) The name and residence of the proprietor of the copyright or any portion thereof.

**DECLARATION**

12. "We hereby declare that the particulars furnished above are true to our knowledge and belief".

13. Nothing in the foregoing rules shall apply to an edition of a book in which no additions or alterations either in the latter-press or in the maps, prints or other engravings, belonging to the edition last preceding, have been made, provided that three copies of the first or later edition of the book were delivered.

14. If the periodicity of publication of a newspaper is changed the declaration made in respect of such newspaper under rule (2) contained in Section 5 shall cease to have effect within the meaning of that section and it shall be necessary for the Printer or Publisher of such newspaper to make a declaration under Section 8 to the effect that he has ceased to the Printer or Publisher thereof and also to make a new declaration under rule (2) contained in Section 5 for publishing the newspaper with the changed periodicity.

C. V. DUTTR

Deputy Secretary to Government

To

The Director, Government Printing Press, Hyderabad for publication of the Notification in the *Andhra Pradesh Gazette.*

The Translator to Government, Hyderabad for furnishing translation of the Notification in Telugu and Urdu to the Director, Printing Press, Hyderabad for publication in the *Andhra Pradesh Gazette.*

The Registrar of Books, Andhra Pradesh, Hyderabad.

The Collectors of District and the Commissioner of Police, Hyderabad.

The Director of Information and Public Relations, Hyderabad.

Copy to Education department.

Copy to Director of Public Instruction, A. P., Hyderabad.

Sd/-

SECTION OFFICER

Annexure-2

## NUMBER OF PRINTING PRESSES AT WORK, NEWSPAPERS, PERIODICALS AND BOOKS REGISTERED

| | | | BOOKS REGISTERED | | | | | | | | | | | |
|---|---|---|---|---|---|---|---|---|---|---|---|---|---|---|
| *SI. No.* | *Year* | *Printing Presses* | *Tel-ugu* | *Hindi* | *Sans-krit* | *Tamil* | *Kann-ada* | *Mala-yalam* | *Marathi* | *Urdu* | *English & European Lan.* | *Bi-lingquil* | *Total* | *News-papers & Periodicals (Titles only)* |
| 1 | 1998-1999 | 2434 | 811 | 4 | 1 | | | | | 24 | 88 | 6 | 934 | 405 |
| 2 | 1999-2000 | 2435 | 2440 | 14 | 10 | - | - | - | - | 35 | 199 | 91 | 2830 | 457 |
| 3 | 2000-2001 | 2420 | 1200 | 13 | 1 | - | - | - | - | 18 | 165 | 11 | 1408 | 413 |
| 4 | 2001-2002 | 2420 | 2652 | 11 | 2 | - | - | - | - | 28 | 207 | 2 | 2902 | 425 |
| 5 | 2002-2003 | – | 1862 | 11 | 2 | - | - | - | - | 30 | 200 | 2 | 3107 | 460 |
| 6 | 2003-2004 | – | 1845 | 45 | - | - | - | - | - | 77 | 369 | - | 2336 | 475 |

*Source: Registrar of Publications, Andhra Pradesh*

## RECEIPT OF PUBLICATIONS UNDER PRESS AND REGISTRATION OF BOOKS ACT, 1867 IN SOUTH INDIA

As per Section 20 (Part/VI) of the Act, Government of Andhra Pradesh has framed rules (Andhra Pradesh Press and Registration of Books Rules, 1960) vide GO MS No.2104 Home (General-A) Department dated 10.10.1960 for overseeing the working of the Act in the State. In GO MS No.235 Home (General-A) Department dated 11.02.1976, Government of A. P. have changed the designation of "Registrar of Books" as "Registrar of Publications". In GO MS No.286 the Director of Public Libraries (DPL) shall be Ex-Officio Registrar of Publications so as to ensure proper implementation of the provisions of the Act in the entire State of Andhra Pradesh. With the help of District Magistrates and Commissioner of Police, Hyderabad City, the Registrar of Publications is implementing the relevant sections of the Act.

In Tamil Nadu and Kerala there is no separate Office of Registrar of Publications. The Departments of Information and Public Relations of the two State Governments are charged with the overseeing the working of the Act and receiving the Publications. In Karnataka, it is the Director, Dept. of Public Libraries, Government of Karnataka oversees the implementation of the Act. The Librarian, State Central Library at Cubbon Park, Bangalore receives the copies of the printed books and other reading materials under the provisions of the P.R.B. Act, 1867. The books received under the provisions of PRB Act, 1867 by the four Southern States for the five years period i.e. 1998-99 to 2002-03 is presented in the following table.

**Table**

| *Name of the State:* | *1998-1999* | *1999-2000* | *2000-2001* | *2001-2002* | *2002-2003* |
|---|---|---|---|---|---|
| Andhra Pradesh | 9342,8 | 30 | 1,408 | 2,902 | 2,107 |
| Karnataka | 2,381 | 3,063 | 3,377 | 2,546 | 3,283 |
| Kerala* | — | — | — | — | — |
| Tamil Nadu | NA | 10.60 | 1,0 | 1,0 | 1,050 |

***Source:*** *The Registrar of Publications, Govt. of A. P., Hyderabad and Director, Dept. of Public Libraries, Govt. of Karnataka, Bangalore, Public Relations Officer (PRO), State Secvretariat, Govt. of Tamil Nadu, Chennai.*

* The Director, Dept. of Information and Public Relations, Govt. of Kerala, Tiruvananthapuram has provided information on the receipt of books under PRB Act, 1867 for the following three years.

**Table**

| 2003-2004 | 2004-2005 | 2005-2006 |
|---|---|---|
| 55 | 54 | 88 |

***Source:*** *Dept. of Information and Public Relations, Government of Kerala*

## LANGUAGE WISE RECEIPT OF PUBLICATIONS

The major languages in which books and other reading materials were being published in addition to English are: Telugu, Kannada, Tamil, Malayalam, Urdu, Sanskrit and Hindi. There may be few exceptions where books might have been published other than these languages. The following tables provide figures of receipt of books year wise / language wise by the four Southern States during the five year period:

**Table : Name of the State: Andhra Pradesh**

| *Language /Year* | *1998-99* | *1999-00* | *2000-01* | *2001-02* | *2002-03* | *Total:* |
|---|---|---|---|---|---|---|
| Telugu | 811 | 2,440 | 1,218 | 2,650 | 1,862 | 8,981 |
| Kannada | — | 01 | — | — | — | 01 |
| Tamil | — | — | — | — | — | — |
| Malayalam | — | — | — | — | — | — |
| Urdu | 24 | 75 | 20 | 28 | 30 | 177 |
| English | 88 | 199 | 145 | 207 | 200 | 839 |
| Sanskrit | 01 | 10 | 01 | 02 | 02 | 16 |
| Hindi | 04 | 14 | 13 | 11 | 11 | 53 |
| Polyglot | 06 | 91 | 11 | 04 | 02 | 114 |
| Total: | 934 | 2,830 | 1,408 | 2,902 | 2,107 | 10,181 |

***Source:*** *Registrar of Publications, Govt. of A.P.Hyderabad.*

From the above Table it is evident that in Telugu, the State Official Language, more number of books have been received during the five year period under study followed by English Language. Urdu, the second State language occupies the third place in respect of number of books received at the Registrar of Publications, Government of A. P. During the year 2001-02, the Office of the Registrar of Publications has received more number of books i.e. 2,902 compared to other years under study. During the five year period, 8981 Telugu language books were received at the Registrar of Publications, Govt. of A. P., followed by 839 in English and 177 in Urdu. The total books received by the Registrar of publications, Govt. of A. P., during the five year period was 10,181.

**Table : Name of the State: KARNATAKA**

| *Language /Year* | *1998-99* | *1999-00* | *2000-01* | *2001-02* | *2002-03* | *Total:* |
|---|---|---|---|---|---|---|
| Telugu | - | 4 | 8 | 7 | 4 | 23 |
| Kannada | 2193 | 2656 | 2693 | 2183 | 2732 | 12,457 |
| Tamil | _ | _ | 6 | 6 | 6 | 16 |
| Malayalam | — | — | 6 | 1 | 2 | 9 |
| Urdu | — | 13 | 16 | 6 | 16 | 51 |
| English | 184 | 358 | 633 | 310 | 487 | 1972 |
| Sanskrit | — | 5 | — | 02 | 01 | 8 |
| Hindi | 04 | 21 | 12 | 14 | 32 | 83 |
| Marathi | — | 6 | 3 | 17 | 5 | 31 |
| Total: | 2381 | 3063 | 3377 | 2546 | 3283 | 14,650 |

***Source:*** *Librarian, State Central Library, Bangalore*

From the above table it is evident that during the five year period, the office of the Librarian, State Central Library has received 12,457 books in Kannada, the State official language, followed by 1972 books in English, 83 in Hindi and 51 Urdu. During the years 2000-2001, the Office has received more books i.e. 3377 than the remaining four years. The total books received during the five year period were 14,650 which appear to be more impressive when compared with Andhra Pradesh, which received 10,181 during the said five year period. It appears that Printers in Karnataka are more responsive and aware of the provisions of PRB Act, 1867. The State Administration was also more vigilant and initiated suitable actions against the erring printers in the State.

**Table : Name of the State: Kerala**

| *Language / Year* | *2003-2004* | *2004-2005* | *2005-2006* | *Total:* |
|---|---|---|---|---|
| Telugu | — | — | — | — |
| Kannada | — | — | — | — |
| Tamil | — | — | — | — |
| Malayalam | 54 | 46 | 85 | 185 |
| Urdu | — | — | — | — |
| English | 01 | 07 | 03 | 11 |
| Sanskrit | — | — | — | — |
| Hindi | — | 01 | — | 01 |
| Total: | 55 | 54 | 88 | 197 |

***Source:*** *Dept. of Information and Public Relations, Govt. of Kerala.*

As stated already the Department of Information and Public Relations, Government of Kerala obliged to provide information for three year period i.e. 2003-04 to 2005-06 instead five year period i.e. 1998-1999 - 2002-2003. As for literacy rate in India is concerned, Kerala is one of the leading States of the Indian Union having near 100% literacy rate. As a corollary the book production in the State also should be more impressive when compared with the other Southern States. But the figures provided by the concerned authority are not encouraging and does not reflect the actual annual book production in State. During the three year period, the Department of Information and Public Relations, Government of Kerala has received 197 books only of which 185 are in Malayalam the State official language, 11 in English and 1 in Hindi. The above table reflects the tardy implementation of PRB Act, 1867 in Kerala and the non-cooperation of printers in the State knowingly or unknowingly. It appears strange that politically, socially and educationally conscious State like Kerala, the actual book production and conforming to the provisions of **PRB** Act, 1867 by the Printers is not reflected in the figures provided by the Government. The reasons for this not so happy state of affairs of bibliographical control in Kerala may be lack of proper Government machinery to oversee the implementation of the provisions of PRB Act, 1867 and lack of cooperation from the Printers. Sukumaran Nair opines that "according to Press and Registration of books Act, 1867 a few publishers are sending copies to the Public Relations Department (PRD), Government of Kerala. In the survey conducted it was found that PRD received 94 books during 2004 and 95 books during 2005. Records of previous years are not readily available. This number is considered to be less than 10% of the annual publications in the State"[9].

The Government of Tamilnadu, it appears, is not maintaining the figures pertaining to language wise breakup of receipt of books under Press and Registration Books Act, 1867. The receipt of books for years 2003-04 to 2006-07 is as follows:

| *Years* | *No. of Books Received:* |
|---|---|
| 2003-2004 | 1300 |
| 2004-2005 | 1250 |
| 2005-2006 | 1350 |
| 2006-2007 | 1848 |

In Tamilnadu more number of books are published annually when compared with other Southern States of India. But the receipt of books under the provisions of PRB Act, 1867 is not encouraging.

## REFERENCES

1. Jules Lari Viere. *Guidelines for Legal Deposit Legislation.* Paris, NESCO, 2000. p.6.

2. M. B. Meshram. Press and Registration of Books Act, 1867. *In Study material for orientation on Press and Registration Act, Delivery of Books Act & Copyright Act.* Nanded, Swamy Ramanand Teerth Marathwada University, 2004, p. 131.

3. *Information Management in the Parliament of India.* New Delhi, Lok Sabha Secretariat, 2000. p. 18.

4. M. B. Meshram. Press & Registration of Books Act, 1867. *In Study material for orientation on Press and Registration Act, Delivery of Books Act & Copyright Act.* Nanded, Swamy Ramanand Teerth Marathwada University, 2004,p.141.

5. Communication dated February 25, 2008 received from Prof. N. R. Satyanarayana, Head, Dept. of Library & Information Science, Lucknow University, Lucknow.

6. Information provide by Ms. Sabita Kundu, Librarian, Techno-India College of Technology, Rajarhat, Kolkata-700 156.

7. The Assam Public Libraries and Information Services Draft Bill, 2006 (submitted by the Committee constituted for drafting the Bill vide Memo No. ETM.29/2002/3-A, dt. Dispur 6.6.2002). *Courtesy*: Dr. Narendra Lahkar, Prof. & Head, Dept. of Library & Information Science, Gauhati University, Guvahati, and Chairman, Drafting Committee.

8. R. Rama Swamy. The National Bibliographical Control. *In National Bibliographical Problems and Perspectives,* ed. by A. A. N. Raju and L. S. Ramaiah. New Delhi, Allied, 2003, pp.87-83.

9. N. Sukumaran Nair. The Delivery of Books and News Papers (Public Libraries) Act, 1954 (Act 27 of 1954) in Kerala. In Regional Seminar : Delivery of Books and Newspapers (Public Libraries) Act, 1954. *Seminar Papers.* Kolkata, National Library, 2006. p.69.

# 6

# RECEIPT OF BOOKS UNDER DELIVERY OF BOOKS AND NEWSPAPERS (PUBIC LIBRARIES) ACT, 1954

As stated already legal deposit in India has it genesis with the enactment of Delivery of Books and Newspapers (Public Libraries) act, 1954 by the Government of India to have a system which ensures the preservations of country's documentary heritage. The said act ensures total coverage through compulsory deposit of a copy of every document published in the Country at the National Library, Kolkata and three designated deposit libraries viz. 1. Connemara Public Library, Chennai, 2. State Central Library, Mumbai and 3. Delhi Public Library, Delhi. The principal objective of the DB Act, 1954 is to "institutionalize a system that helps the preservation of the country's cultural and intellectual heritage embodied mainly in readable materials but also in lithographed and manuscript forms. Thus the system of compulsory deposit of a copy of nearly every thing published in the country to the public libraries ensures total coverage of all published documents that can be preserved for posterity"[1].

As per the provisions of the act a publisher has to send a copy of every publication free of cost to the National Library and the three designated libraries by registered post. The following tables in the succeeding paras provide an idea as to the number of books received by the four libraries during the five year period i.e. 1998-99 to 2002-03.

## RECEIPT OF BOOKS AT THE NATIONAL LIBRARY:

It has been observed that the receipt of books at the National Library, Kolkata under DB Act, 1954 is not encouraging. The reason for this state of affairs is lack of cooperation from the publishers. It has been estimated that not more than 30% to 40% of the books published in the Country are deposited at the National Library, Kolkata under the provisions of the DB Act, 1954. Mandal observes that "the reasons for non-submission of books are many. Some publishers especially the new in the trade are not aware of the obligations. It is estimated that the number of registered publishers exceeds 11,000. But most of them are medium or small concerns. It is observed that more than 50% of the total number belongs to individual publishing concerns. Not more than 10% or so are members of any organized association or guild of publishers. This makes difficult for the National Library to get information about their publications and make them aware of the legal deposit. It is also observed that the publishers do not find any incentive to submit a book because submission does not lead to increase sale of books"[2].

Another important reason for this state of affairs is the "seven book syndrome". It means that as per the provisions of Press and Registration of Books Act, 1867 every printer has to submit three copies of each of the publication to the Registrar of Publications / Department of Information and Public Relations or any other designated office of the concerned State Government. In addition as per the provisions of Delivery of Books and Newspapers (Public Libraries) Act, 1954 every publisher has to submit one copy to the National Library and a copy of each to the three designated recipient libraries. Thus the burden of sending *seven copies* of each of the publications by registered post to the recipient agencies that too bearing the postal expenses by the Printer / Publisher is another important discouraging factor. Therefore, the two acts i.e. PRB Act, 1867 an DB Act, 1954 mostly implemented in breach.

## NUMBER OF BOOKS RECEIVED AT THE NATIONAL LIBRARY

Abuzar stated that "the highest number of publications received in a year in the National Library was 37,311 in the year 1956-57, the first year of the receipt after the amendment of the Act. But an analysis of the yearly receipt of books at the National Library under the Act reveals that, there was a gradual decrease in it. The average receipt of books in the library in 1950's it was 26,000, in 1960's it was 19,000, in 1970's it was 18,000 and in 1980's it was 16000"[3]. The receipt of books at the National Library, Kolkata and the three designated depository libraries for a five year period i.e. 1998-99 to 2002-03 is given below:

**Table : Books received by the four Deposit libraries during the five year period**

| *Name of the Library/Year* | *1998-99* | *1999-00* | *2000-01* | *2001-02* | *2002-03* | *Total:* |
|---|---|---|---|---|---|---|
| National Library, New Delhi | 15,922 | 20,012 | 19,961 | 18,212 | 20,309 | 95,252 |
| Connemara Public Library, Chennai | 7,745 | 9,612 | 10,544 | 12,392 | 12,893 | 53,186 |
| State Central Library, Mumbai | 7,840 | 10,653 | 12,671 | 12,511 | 12,537 | 56,212 |
| Delhi Public Library, Delhi | 12,388 | 10,525 | 12,51 | 13,383 | 12,487 | 61,244 |

***Source:*** *National Library, Kolkata*

According to Federation of Publishers' and Book Sellers' Association in India (FPBA) the annual book production in the Country is about 60,000 titles. This may not be a correct figure. As many of the publishers especially Author publishers are not members of this Association. If we consider that 60,000 as a base figure and can be depended upon, the National Library receives about 'one third' of the total book production as per the provisions under DB Act, 1954. The receipt of books at the National Library does not reflect the correct picture obtaining in the country as to the number of books published annually. During the five year period National Library received 92,252 books. On an average, the National Library received 18,450 books per annum which is almost one third of the total annual book production in the country on the basis of the figure of 60,000 arrived at by the Federation of Publishers and Book Sellers' Association in India.

## RECEIPT OF BOOKS BY THE DEPOSITORY LIBRARIES

As per the provisions of DB Act-1954, and the rules made there under the three depository libraries i.e., 1. The Connemara Public Library, Chennai, 2. The State Central Library, Mumbai and 3.The Delhi Public Library, New Delhi have been designated as depository libraries to receive a copy of each of the publications emanating from the Country.

The preceding **Table** provides figures as to the receipt of publications during the five-year period i.e. 1998-99 to 2002-03.

If we observe the figures provided for in the preceding **Table,** it is evident that National Library has been receiving more number of books than the designated three deposit libraries. Of the three deposit libraries, Delhi Public Library has been receiving more number of books than the remaining two deposit libraries at Chennai and Mumbai. During the five year period Delhi Public Library received 61,244 books followed by State Central Library, Mumbai 56,212 and Connemara Public Library 53,186.On an average Connemara Public Library, Chennai, State Central Library, Mumbai, and Delhi Public Library have received 10,637; 11,242 and 12,544 books respectively during the five year period. Whereas the annual receipt of book on an average during the five-year period at the National Library was 18,450. But even this higher receipt of books by the National Library than the three deposit libraries is only one third of the total books published annually in the Country.

Ramachandran analyzed the figures pertaining to the receipt of books by the four libraries for the years 1992-93 to 2003-04 i.e. twelve year period and observed that "National Library, Kolkata has been receiving comparatively higher number of books than the other three libraries. The Annual receipt of the Connemara Public Library, Chennai, State Central Library, Mumbai and Delhi Public Library, New Delhi on an average has remained around 8000,9,500 and 13,000 and whereas the annual receipt of the National Library on an average was around 16,000. Even the highest receipt under Delivery of Books Act by the National Library stands to be one third even lesser than the total number of books published annually in India. The partial success in receipt under the Act suggests a complete overhaul of the Act and its implementation"[4].

## LANGUAGE WISE RECEIPT OF BOOKS BY THE FOUR RECIPIENT LIBRARIES

During the five year period i.e. 1998-99 to 2002-03 the four recipient libraries under DB Act, 1954 viz. National Library, Kolkata, Connemara Public Library Chennai, State Central Library, Mumbai and Delhi Public Library, Delhi have received books in the major South Indian Languages viz. Telugu, Kannada, Tamil, Malayalam and Urdu and also from other Indian languages.

During the five year period, the National Library, Kolkata received 9986 books in 1998-99 followed by 12337 in 1999-2K, 11702 in 2000-2001,14121 in 2001-02 and 13814 in 2002-03. Likewise Connemara Public Librry, Chennai received 6592 in 1998-99 followed by 4988 in 1999-2K, 6064 in 2000-01,7189 in 2001-02 and 12884 in 2002-03. The State Central Library, Mumbai received 6004 books in 1998-99 followedby 5783 in 1999-2K, 10125 in 2000-01 and 9752 in 2001-02. The Delhi Public Library received

**Table : Language Wise Receipt of Books Under DB Act, 1954 by the Four Receipent Libraries**

| *Year* | *Name of the Library* | *Telugu* | *Kann-ada* | *Tamil* | *Mala-yalam* | *Urdu* | *Engl-ish* | *Sans-krit* | *Hindi* | *Others* | *Total* |
|---|---|---|---|---|---|---|---|---|---|---|---|
| | National Library, Kolkata | 576 | 793 | 1929 | 368 | 217 | 4529 | 106 | 1591 | 76 | 9986 |
| 1998-1999 | Connemara Public Library, Chennai | 129 | 218 | 2943 | 333 | 150 | 2116 | 35 | 642 | 26 | 6592 |
| | State Central Library, Mumbai | 77 | 280 | 1632 | 129 | 213 | 2616 | 152 | 847 | 58 | 6004 |
| | Delhi Public Library, Delhi | 158 | 133 | 2416 | 89 | 390 | 3467 | - | 4574 | - | 11227 |
| | National Library, Kolkata | 484 | 966 | 2620 | 860 | 245 | 5471 | 74 | 1514 | 103 | 12337 |
| 1999-2000 | Connemara Public Library, Chennai | 107 | 175 | 107 | 224 | 88 | 3403 | 25 | 840 | 19 | 4988 |
| | State Central Library, Mumbai | 139 | 281 | 139 | 235 | 136 | 3043 | 24 | 1262 | 524 | 5783 |
| | Delhi Public Library, Delhi | 36 | 138 | 36 | 78 | 279 | 3947 | - | 3024 | ~ | 7538 |

| *Year* | *Name of the Library* | *Telugu* | *Kannada* | *Tamil* | *Malayalam* | *Urdu* | *English* | *Sanskrit* | *Hindi* | *Others* | *Total* |
|---|---|---|---|---|---|---|---|---|---|---|---|
| | National Library, Kolkata | 452 | 656 | 2903 | 603 | 201 | 6734 | 99 | 2043 | 11 | 11702 |
| 2000-2001 | Connemara Public Library, Chennai | 154 | 197 | - | 320 | 84 | 21241 | 24 | 1145 | 19 | 6064 |
| | State Central Library, Mumbai | 229 | 293 | 839 | 384 | 98 | 3533 | 38 | 1599 | 112 | 10125 |
| | Delhi Public Library, Delhi | 145 | 120 | 512 | 327 | 292 | 5085 | 223 | 4331 | — | 10935 |
| | National Library, Kolkata | 360 | 590 | 2823 | 310 | 31 | 7309 | 138 | 2280 | .. | 14121 |
| 2001-2002 | Connemara Public Library, Chennai | 143 | 239 | - | 294 | 188 | 4667 | 52 | 1578 | 28 | 7189 |
| | State Central Library, Mumbai | 144 | 156 | 2651 | 98 | 143 | 4627 | 45 | 1744 | 64 | 9752 |
| | Delhi Public Library, Delhi | 152 | 397 | 1237 | 416 | 360 | 4749 | 132 | 4612 | - | 12055 |

| *Year* | *Name of the Library* | *Telugu* | *Kann-ada* | *Tamil* | *Mala-yalam* | *Urdu* | *Engl-ish* | *Sans-krit* | *Hindi* | *Others* | *Total* |
|---|---|---|---|---|---|---|---|---|---|---|---|
| | National Library, Kolkata | 365 | 683 | 2966 | 401 | 357 | 6625 | 145 | 2272 | - | 13814 |
| 2002-2003 | Connemara Public Library, Chennai | 171 | 174 | 4015 | 365 | 98 | 5628 | 26 | 1117 | 1290 | 12884 |
| | State Central Library, Mumbai | — | — | — | — | — | — | — | — | — | — |
| | Delhi Public Library, Delhi | — | — | — | — | — | — | — | — | — | — |

***Source:*** *National Library, Kolkata*

11227 books in 1998-99 followedby 7538in 1999-2K, 10935 in 2000-01 and12055 in 2001-02. Except in the year 1998-99, the National Library, Kolkata has received more number of books than the remaining three depository libraries.

## LANGUAGE WISE RECEIPT OF BOOKS (UNDER DB ACT, 1954) BY THE CONNEMARA PUBLIC LIBRARY, CHENNAI

The following table provides figures of receipt of books language wise during the years 1968-2005 i.e. more than three and half decades by the Connemara Public Library, Chennai which is the designated library. From the Table it can be concluded that English Language books occupy prime position (1,06,659) followedby Tamil (67,033), Hindi (43,771), Marathi (27,928), Malayalam (15,416), Kannada (12,722), Bengali (11,406) and Telugu (8,074). During the span of three and half decades the library has received 3,19,632 books. During the years 1976-85 the library has received highest number of books (1,04,264) when compared with the years 1968-75,1986-95 and 1996-2005. From among the South Indian languages Tamil language books (67,033) occupy prime position followed by Malayalam (15,416), Kannada (12,722) and Telugu (8,074).

**Table**

| *S. No.* | *Language:* | *1968-75* | *1976-85* | *1986-95* | *1996-2005* | *Total:* |
|---|---|---|---|---|---|---|
| 1 | English | 2,176 | 39,930 | 28,864 | 35,689 | 1,06,659 |
| 2 | Tamil | 4,618 | 13,581 | 16,267 | 32,567 | 67,033 |
| 3 | Kannada | 2,368 | 5,196 | 3,354 | 1,804 | 12,722 |
| 4 | Malayalam | 3,411 | 5,836 | 3,217 | 2,952 | 15,416 |
| 5 | Telugu | 2,376 | 2,529 | 1,831 | 1,338 | 8,074 |

| *S. No.* | *Language:* | *1968-75* | *1976-85* | *1986-95* | *1996-2005* | *Total:* |
|---|---|---|---|---|---|---|
| 6 | Assamese | 393 | 264 | 234 | 40 | 931 |
| 7 | Bengali | 2,412 | 3,536 | 3,357 | 2,101 | 11,406 |
| 8 | Guarathi | 2,230 | 4,673 | 3,021 | 1,780 | 11,704 |
| 9 | Hindi | 9,763 | 14,719 | 10,227 | 9,062 | 43,771 |
| 10 | Marathi | 4,913 | 9,494 | 7,291 | 6,230 | 27,928 |
| 11 | Oriya | 341 | 575 | 218 | 168 | 1,302 |
| 12 | Punjabi | 860 | 1,242 | 1,274746 | | 4,122 |
| 13 | Sanskrit | 721 | 988 | 390 | 316 | 2,415 |
| 14 | Urdu | 921 | 1,264 | 1,600 | 1,029 | 4814 |
| 15 | Other Languages | 96 | 437 | 516 | 286 | 1335 |
| | TOTAL | 57,187 | 1,04,264 | 81,661 | 96,108 | 319,632 |

***Source:*** *Conemara Public Library - Annual Reports*[1]

English language publications occupy dominant position. The book publication in other languages, as per the above Table, is not encouraging. The book production in the Indian languages has to go a long way to compete with English language publications and to occupy the prime position. But the above Table may not reflect the actual publication scene of Indian Publications as many of the publishers both commercial and author do not comply with the provisions of DB Act, 1954 deliberately or out of ignorance.

## STATE WISE RECEIPT OF BOOKS BY THE NATIONAL LIBRARY

As per the provisions under section 3 of the Delivery of Books and Newspapers (Public Libraries) Act, 1954 a publisher has to deliver at his own expenses a copy of the book to the National Library at Kolkata and one such copy to each of the other three public libraries. The National Library at Kolkata has been receiving copies of publications from the publishers of the Country.

The following Table provides figures of receipt of books from various states and Union Territories of India for a period of four years.

**Table**

| *Name of the State:* | *1998-1999* | *1999-2000* | *2000-2001* | *2001-2002* | *2002-2003* |
|---|---|---|---|---|---|
| Andaman & Nicobar | 5 | 5 | — | 13 | |
| Andhra Pradesh | 630 | 509 | — | 488 | 433 |
| Arunachal Pradesh | 17 | 18 | — | 25 | — |
| Assam | 395 | 809 | — | 452 | 370 |
| Bihar | 366 | 378 | — | 212 | 241 |
| Chandigarh | 133 | 39 | — | 43 | 101 |
| Chathisgadh | — | — | — | — | 4 |
| Dadra & Nagar Haveli | — | — | — | 2 | — |
| Delhi | 3186 | 3772 | — | 5186 | 3252 |
| Goa | 57 | 74 | — | 98 | 40 |
| Gujarat | 596 | 967 | — | 495 | 69 |
| Haryana | 33 | 37 | — | 46 | 83 |
| Himachal Pradesh | 39 | 45 | — | 25 | 24 |
| Jammu & Kashmir | 13 | 16 | — | 15 | 25 |
| Jharkhand | — | — | — | — | — |
| Karnataka | 1012 | 1177 | — | 789 | 180 |
| Kerala | 520 | 1002 | — | 433 | — |
| Lakshdweep | 365 | — | — | 3 | — |
| Madhya Pradesh | 285 | 306 | — | 119 | 134 |
| Maharashtra | 1658 | 1610 | — | 1329 | 2013 |
| Manipur | 14 | 13 | — | 12 | — |
| Meghalaya | 17 | 20 | — | 37 | 5 |
| Mizoram | 3 | 6 | — | 16 | — |
| Nagaland | — | 1 | — | 7 | — |
| Orissa | 1999 | 3010 | — | 319 | 1882 |

| *Name of the State:* | *1998-1999* | *1999-2000* | *2000-2001* | *2001-2002* | *2002-2003* |
|---|---|---|---|---|---|
| Panjab | 222 | 326 | — | 334 | 589 |
| Pondichery | 86 | 74 | — | 107 | 157 |
| Rajasthan | 138 | 77 | — | 300 | 126 |
| Sikkim | 2 | 4 | — | 25 | — |
| Tamilnadu | 2080 | 2825 | — | 3274 | 3695 |
| Tripura | 13 | 12 | — | 37 | 12 |
| Uttaranchal | — | — | — | — | 316 |
| Uttar Pradesh | 472 | 504 | — | 979 | 167 |
| West Bengal | 1949 | 2376 | — | 2992 | 2763 |
| **Total:** | 15922 | 20,012 | — | 18212 | 17613 |

***Source:*** *National Library, Kolkata*

From the above Table it can be concluded that from among the States of India, the National Library has received more number of books during the four year period from Delhi (15,396) followed by Tamilnadu (11,874), West Bengal (10,080) and Maharashtra (6,610). It is obvious that Delhi has become an import book publishing Centre not only for India but also the entire World. This is because major English Publishers both foreign and Indian and stationed at Delhi. During the four year period the National Library has received a total number of 15,922 (1998-99) 20,012 (199-2000), 18,212 (2001-2002) and 17,613 (2002-2003) from the States and Union Territories of India. But these figures do not reflect the actual annual book production in the Country.

## LANGUAGE WISE RECEIPT OF BOOKS BY THE NATIONAL LIBRARY

The following Table provides figures for language wise receipt of books by the National Library under Delivery of Books and Newspapers (Public Libraries)

Act, 1954.

**Table: Language wise receipt of books by the National Library, Kolkata**

| *Language wise Books received* | *1998-1999* | *1999-2000* | *2000-2001* | *2001-2002* | *2002-2003* | *Total:* |
|---|---|---|---|---|---|---|
| Assamese | 355 | 780 | 637 | 420 | 530 | 2722 |
| Bengali | 1452 | 1794 | 1986 | 2001 | 2028 | 3261 |
| English | 4529 | 5471 | 6734 | 7309 | 6625 | 30668 |
| Gujarati | 503 | 908 | 336 | 457 | 387 | 2591 |
| Hindi | 1591 | 1514 | 2043 | 2280 | 2272 | 9700 |
| Kannada | 793 | 966 | 656 | 590 | 683 | 3688 |
| Kashmiri | — | — | — | — | — | — |
| Malayalam | 368 | 850 | 603 | 310 | 401 | 2532 |
| Marathi | 1185 | 1202 | 1266 | 738 | 1389 | 5782 |
| Oriya | 1941 | 2784 | 1708 | 152 | 1733 | 8318 |
| Panjabi | 303 | 291 | 326 | 301 | 363 | 1584 |
| Sanskrit | 105 | 74 | 99 | 138 | 145 | 561 |
| Sindhi | 57 | — | — | — | — | 57 |
| Tamil | 1929 | 2620 | 2903 | 2823 | 2966 | 13241 |
| Telugu | 575 | 484 | 452 | 360 | 365 | 2236 |
| Urdu | 217 | 245 | 201 | 311 | 357 | 1331 |
| Other Languages | 19 | 29 | 11 | 22 | 65 | 146 |
| Total: | 15922 | 20012 | 19961 | 18212 | 20309 | 94419 |

***Source:*** *National Library, Kolkata.*

The above Table shows that between the years 1998-99 to 2002-2003 i.e. for a period of five years the National Library received 15,922 (1998-99), 20,012 (1999-2000), 19,961 (2000-2001), 18,212 (2001-2002) and 20,309 (2002-2003) books covering major Indian languages. During this five year period, the publications in English touches 30,668 the highest figure when compared with other Indian languages followed by Tamil 13,241, Hindi, 9,700, Bengali 9,261 and Oriya 8,318. The National Library received more number of books in English during the five year period than any other Indian languages. During the five year period a total 94,419 books were received at the National Library of which English language books account for one third of the total publications. Of the major South Indian Languages Tamil books occupy the prime position accounting 13,241 followed by Kannada 3688, Malayalam 2532 and Telugu 2236. The three South Indian Languages i.e. Telugu, Kannada and Malayalam have to go a long way to catch up with Tamil language in the matter of publications and their receipt at the National Library and the other three designated libraries.

## REFERENCES

1. R. Ramachandran. The Delivery of Books and Newspapers (Public Libraries) Act, 1954 and its operation. Paper presented to Workshop on Delivery of Books Act & Conservation of Documentary Heritage. Organized by the National Library of India, Kolkata and Salarjung Museum Library, Hyderabad, Feb. 24-25,2002. Brochure p.4.
2. S. Mandal. National Library of India. In Regional Seminar on Delivery of Books and Newspapers (Public Libraries) Act, 1954. Jan. 24,2006. Seminar Papers. Kolkata, National Library, 2006. pp. 14-15.
3. Syed Abuzar. National Bibliographical Control and Legal Deposit in India: An overview. In *Information Management in Knowledge Society*. Kolkata, IASLI, 2005. p.425.*Receipt of Books Under Delivery* ... 95
4. R. Ramachandran. The 50 years of the Delivery of Books and Newspapers Act (1954). In Regional Seminar on D. B. Act, 1954. Seminar Papers. Kolkata, National Library, 2006. p.94.

5. Quoted by Prof. R. Ramesh Babu and Dr. Ramesha in their article *Delivery of Books (Public Libraries) and Newspapers Act of 1954 with Special Reference to Tamilnadu State.* In Delivery of Books and Newspapers (Public Libraries) Act, 1954 Seminar Papers. Ed. by Prof. C. R. Karisiddappa et al. Dharwad, DLIS, Karnatak University. 2006. p.54.

# 7

# Receipt of Books from the Southern States at the National Library Under DB Act, 1954

The publication activity for five year period 1998-2003 in the four Southern States viz: Andhra Pradesh, Tamilnadu, Karnataka and Kerala in the major South Indian languages viz. Telugu, Tamil, Kannada and Malayalam including other languages such as: Urdu, English, Sanskrit and Hindi is shown in the following **Table.** During the year 1998-99 the National Library, Kolkata received a total of 614 titles from Andhra Pradesh followed by 2080 from Tamilnadu, 960 from Karnataka and 528 from Kerala. In the year 1999-2000 the receipt of books at National Library was 509 (Andhra Pradesh), 2825 (Tamilnadu), 1137 (Karnataka) and 1002 (Kerala). The figures for the year 2000-2001 were not available. During the year 2001 -2002, the receipt of books at National Library from Andhra

Pradesh was (588), Tamilnadu (3274), Karnataka (783) and Kerala (433). In the year 2002-2003, the National Library received 433 from Andhra Pradesh, 3692 (Taimilnadu), 168 (Karnataka) and 922 (Kerala). In the four year period mentioned above the National Library received largest number of books from Tamilnadu (11871) followed by Karnataka (3048), Kerala (2885) and Andhra Pradesh (2144). From the four Southern States the receipt of books from Tamilnadu at the National Library is noteworthy. The reason for this positive aspect perhaps may be the designation of Connemara Public Library, Chennai as one of the recipient libraries under DB Act, 1954. The other reason may be that the Book Publishers in Tamilnadu are aware of the provisions of the DB Act, 1954 and their obligation to send a copy of every publication to the National Library and other three depository libraries. Another reason may be that the publication activity is more vigorous than the remaining three States of Southern India.

## LANGUAGE WISE RECEIPT OF BOOKS BY THE NATIONAL LIBRARY

The major languages of the four Southern States are Telugu, Tamil, Kannada and Malayalam. In addition to these languages books are published in English, Urdu, Hindi and Sanskrit in the four Southern States with few exceptions to other languages. During the five year period under study i.e. 1998-1999 to 2002-2003 that National Library received a total of 2236 Telugu Books, 3688 Kannada, 13,241 Tamil, 2532 Malayalam, 1331 Urdu, 30,668 English, 561 Sanskrit and 9700 Hindi books. The breakup figure for the five-year period is presented in the following Table. As for the four South Indian Languages: Telugu, Tamil,

**Table : Yearwise / Statewise / Language wise Receipt of Books Under DB Act, 1954 By The National Library, Kolkata**

| Year | Name of the Library | Telugu | Kannada | Tamil | Malayalam | Urdu | English | Sanskrit | Hindi | Others | Total |
|---|---|---|---|---|---|---|---|---|---|---|---|
| | Andhra Pradesh | 484 | — | — | — | — | 115 | 3 | 12 | — | 614 |
| 1998- | Taminadu | 35 | 2 | 185 | 1 | 2 | 184 | - | - | — | 2080 |
| 1999 | Karnataka | 15 | 780 | 6 | - | 1 | 146 | — | 3 | — | 960 |
| | Kerala | 22 | — | 15 5 | 365 | 10 | 119 | ~ | 7 | ~ | 528 |
| | Andhra Pradesh | 385 | - | 3 | - | 9 | 98 | 5 | 9 | — | 509 |
| 1999- | Taminadu | 29 | 4 | 256 | 2 | 1 | 220 | 4 | 1 | - | 2825 |
| 2000 | Karnataka | 32 | 939 | 4 | — | — | 147 | 6 | 2 | — | 1137 |
| | Kerala | 15 | 6 | 11 6 | 843 | - | 127 | 1 | 4 | — | 1002 |
| | Andhra Pradesh | | | | | | | | | | |
| 2000- | Taminadu | | | | Not Available | | | | | | |
| 2001 | Karnataka | | | | | | | | | | |
| | Kerala | | | | | | | | | | |

| Year | Name of the Library | Telugu | Kannada | Tamil | Malayalam | Urdu | English | Sanskrit | Hindi | Others | Total |
|---|---|---|---|---|---|---|---|---|---|---|---|
| | Andhra Pradesh | 315 | — | 5 | — | 12 | 154 | — | 2 | — | 588 |
| 2001- | Taminadu | 9 | 1 | 275 | — | 4 | 479 | 10 | 17 | — | 3274 |
| 2002 | Karnataka | 12 | 569 | 4 | — | 9 | 176 | 1 | 2 | — | 783 |
| | Kerala | 4 | — | 14 | 310 | — | 104 | 12 | 3 | — | 433 |
| | Andhra Pradesh | 35 | — | 8 | — | 16 | 73 | — | 1 | — | 433 |
| 2002- | Taminadu | 21 | — | 305 | — | 3 | 597 | 7 | 10 | — | 3692 |
| 2003 | Karnataka | 17 | — | 7 | 3 | — | 83 | 1 | 43 | — | 168 |
| | Kerala | 7 | — | 21 | 870 | — | 34 | — | — | — | 922 |

*Source: National Library, Kolkata*

Kannada and Malayalam are concerned 95% of the total publications for the five year period mentioned above have published from within their respective State boundaries. From among the four South Indian languages publications, Tamil occupy the prime position (13,241) followed by Kannda (3688), Malayalam (2532) and Telugu 2236). Tamil is far ahead of the other three sister languages. Among the other non-South Indian languages, the publications in English occupy first position totaling 30,668 books followed by Hindi (9700), Urdu (1331) and Sanskrit (561) during the five year period.

In the year 1998-99 the National Library has received 575 Telugu books followed by 484 in 1999-2000, 452 in 2000-01, 360 in 2001-02 and 365 in 2002-03. Like wise 793 Kannada books were received by the National Library during the year 1998-99 followed by 966 in 1999-2000, 656 in 2000-2001, 590 in 2001-02 and 683 in 2002-03.

As stated already books in Tamil language occupy the first position among the four south Indian languages. During the year 1998-99, the National Library received 1929 Tamil books in 1998-99 followed by 2620 in 1999-2000, 2903 in 2000-01, 2823 in 2001-02 and 2966 in 2002-03. Of the 2620 Tamil books in 1999-2000, the National Library received 3 books from Andhra Pradesh, 11 from Kernataka, 6 from Kerala, 34 from Pondichery and 2564 from Tamilnadu which forms a lion's share.

During the year 2000-01, the National Library received 2903 Tamil books. Of this total 4 books from Andhra Pradesh, 5 from Kerala, 12 from Karnataka, 39 from Pondicherry and 2840 from Tamilnadu. Likewise during the year 2001-02 out of 2823 books in Tamil, the National Library received 3 from Andhra

Pradesh, 4 from Kerala, 14 from Karnataka, 43 from Pondicherry and 2754 from Tamilnadu. During the year 2002-03 the National Library received 2,966 Tamil books of which 6 from Andhra Pradesh, 4 from Kerala, 17 from Karnataka, 61 from Pondicherry and 2871 from Tamilnadu. The language wise receipt of books by the National Library is shown in the following Table.

**Table : Language wise receipt of books by the National Library, Kolkata under DB Act, 1954 For the years 1998-99 to 2002-2003**

| *Language /Year* | *1998-99* | *1999-00* | *2000-01* | *2001-02* | *2002-03* | *Total:* |
|---|---|---|---|---|---|---|
| Telugu | 575 | 484 | 452 | 360 | 365 | 2236 |
| Kannada | 793 | 966 | 656 | 590 | 683 | 3688 |
| Tamil | 1929 | 2620 | 2903 | 2823 | 2966 | 13241 |
| Malayalam | 368 | 850 | 603 | 310 | 401 | 2532 |
| Urdu | 217 | 245 | 201 | 311 | 357 | 1331 |
| English | 4529 | 5471 | 6734 | 7309 | 6625 | 30668 |
| Sanskrit | 105 | 74 | 99 | 138 | 145 | 561 |
| Hindi | 1591 | 1514 | 2043 | 2280 | 2272 | 9700 |

***Source:*** *National Library, Kolkata*

The data pertaining to State wise beak-up for the other South Indian languages is not available.

## LANGUAGE WISE / SUBJECT WISE RECEIPT OF BOOKS BY THE NATIONAL LIBRARY

During the five year period under study i.e. 1998-99 to 2002-03, the National Library has received books under various broad subject fields such as Generalia, Philosophy, Religion, Social Sciences, Language, Sciences, Technology, Arts, Literature and History and Geography in all the major Indian languages. As for the South India is concerned the National Library has received books under the broad subject fields mentioned above in the major South Indian languages such as: Telugu, Kannada, Tamil and Malayalam. The following **Table** indicates the year wise / language wise / subject wise receipts of books during the five year period 1999-99 to 2002-2003 by the National Library. Literatures of these four languages occupy the prime position.

Of the four South Indian Languages, literature of Tamil language occupies the prime position. During the year 1998-99,1125 books were published in Tamil literature followed by 1663 in 999-2000,1886 in 2000-2001,1782 in 2001-02 and 1821 in 2002-03.

In the remaining three languages also i.e., Telugu, Kannada and Malayalam, books on literature occupy the prime position. During the year 1998-99,365 books were received at the National Library on Telugu literature followed by 318 in 1999-2000; 285 in 2000-2001, 226 in 2001-2002 and 232 in 2002-03.

Books on Kannada literature were not lagging behind Tamil and Telugu literatures. During the year 1998-91,377 books on Kannada literature were received at the National Library followed by 540 in 1999-2000, 329 in 2000-2001, 321 in 2001-2002 and 423 in 2002-2003. Malayalam language also contributed significantly to produce good number of books on Malayalam literature. During the year 1998-99, the National Library has received 276 books on Malayalam literature followed by 818 in 1999-2000; 402 in 2000-01; 180 in 2001-02 and 220 in 2002-03.

In addition to the above mentioned four South Indian languages, National Library has received books from other languages such as: Urdu, English, Sanskrit and Hindi. The figures pertaining to the ten major subject fields in these four languages were presented

**Table :Year wise / Language wise / Subject wise receipt of books by the National Library, Kolkata under DB Act, 1954 for the years 1998-99 to 2002-2003**

| Year | Languages | Gener-era | Philo-sophy | Reli-gion | Social Science | Lang-uage | Science | Techn-ology | Arts | Litera-ture | History & Geogr-aphy | Total |
|---|---|---|---|---|---|---|---|---|---|---|---|---|
| | Telugu | 9 | 27 | 80 | 25 | 12 | 32 | 8 | 5 | 365 | 12 | 575 |
| | Kannada | 35 | 3 | 59 | 61 | 9 | 13 | 46 | 84 | 377 | 106 | 793 |
| 1998- | Tamil | 157 | 132 | 82 | 89 | 22 | 56 | 93 | 24 | 1125 | 149 | 1929 |
| 99 | Malayalam | 3 | 9 | 9 | 26 | 3 | 2 | 8 | 1 | 276 | 31 | 368 |
| | Urdu | 9 | — | 19 | 4 | 13 | 3 | 6 | — | 121 | 42 | 217 |
| | English | 183 | 100 | 243 | 2131 | 138 | 507 | 480 | 462 | 218 | 67 | 4529 |
| | Sanskrit | 1 | 24 | 31 | 3 | 16 | 1 | — | — | 29 | — | 105 |
| | Hindi | 30 | 88 | 99 | 287 | 17 | 41 | 60 | 26 | 816 | 127 | 1591 |
| | Telugu | 6 | 21 | 68 | 15 | 9 | 27 | 4 | 3 | 318 | 13 | 484 |
| | Kannada | 26 | 16 | 74 | 59 | 9 | 12 | 32 | 53 | 540 | 145 | 966 |
| 1999- | Tamil | 160 | 142 | 58 | 58 | 62 | 93 | 168 | 46 | 1663 | 170 | 2620 |
| 00 | Malayalam | - | 2 | 12 | 1 | - | 5 | 3 | - | 818 | 9 | 850 |
| | Urdu | 2 | — | 19 | — | 8 | 6 | 9 | 1 | 128 | 72 | 245 |
| | English | 377 | 191 | 458 | 2357 | 126 | 475 | 455 | 171 | 467 | 398 | 5471 |

| *Year* | *Languages* | *Gener-era* | *Philo-sophy* | *Reli-gion* | *Social Science* | *Lang-uage* | *Science* | *Techn-ology* | *Arts* | *Litera-ture* | *History & Geogr-aphy* | *Total* |
|---|---|---|---|---|---|---|---|---|---|---|---|---|
| | Sanskrit | 1 | 5 | 17 | — | 11 | 1 | 7 | 2 | 19 | 1 | 74 |
| | Hindi | 16 | 159 | 118 | 272 | 23 | 47 | 43 | 29 | 688 | 119 | 1514 |
| | Telugu | 7 | 11 | 52 | 22 | 8 | 39 | 9 | 5 | 285 | 17 | 452 |
| | Kannada | 33 | 17 | 38 | 57 | 16 | 16 | 19 | 19 | 329 | 112 | 656 |
| 2000- | Tamil | 173 | 142 | 63 | 54 | 51 | 102 | 177 | 31 | 1886 | 224 | 2903 |
| 01 | Malayalam | 4 | 2 | 110 | 6 | 5 | 8 | 21 | 3 | 402 | 42 | 603 |
| | Urdu | — | — | 7 | 8 | 5 | 10 | 11 | 15 | 110 | 35 | 201 |
| | English | 316 | 266 | 552 | 1346 | 114 | 224 | 524 | 174 | 518 | 282 | 4316 |
| | Sanskrit | 2 | 14 | 43 | 2 | 7 | — | — | 3 | 25 | 3 | 99 |
| | Hindi | 28 | 114 | 121 | 253 | 32 | 57 | 64 | 35 | 1093 | 246 | 2043 |
| | Telugu | 5 | 18 | 46 | 19 | 6 | 22 | 5 | 2 | 226 | 11 | 360 |
| | Kannada | 60 | 11 | 39 | 33 | 10 | 7 | 17 | 15 | 321 | 77 | 590 |
| 2001- | Tamil | 208 | 192 | 75 | 32 | 46 | 113 | 154 | 27 | 1782 | 194 | 2823 |
| 02 | Malayalam | 4 | 3 | 60 | 6 | 3 | 4 | 15 | 5 | 180 | 30 | 310 |
| | Urdu | 1 | 3 | 22 | 9 | 11 | 6 | 10 | — | 171 | 78 | 311 |

| Year | Languages | Gener-era | Philo-sophy | Reli-gion | Social Science | Lang-uage | Science | Techn-ology | Arts | Litera-ture | History & Geogr-aphy | Total |
|---|---|---|---|---|---|---|---|---|---|---|---|---|
| | English | 611 | 220 | 331 | 1495 | 220 | 359 | 462 | 233 | 526 | 379 | 4836 |
| | Sanskrit | 4 | 21 | 29 | 3 | 14 | 2 | 5 | — | 57 | 3 | 138 |
| | Hindi | 46 | 107 | 84 | 174 | 40 | 49 | 50 | 24 | 1485 | 221 | 2280 |
| | Telugu | 3 | 15 | 51 | 18 | 5 | 25 | 3 | 1 | 232 | 12 | 365 |
| | Kannada | 10 | 14 | 55 | 20 | 12 | 8 | 22 | 7 | 423 | 116 | 683 |
| 2002- | Tamil | 232 | 171 | 62 | 45 | 32 | 128 | 169 | 37 | 1821 | 269 | 2966 |
| 03 | Malayalam | 10 | 26 | 35 | 30 | 6 | 10 | 20 | 8 | 220 | 36 | 401 |
| | Urdu | 5 | 7 | 44 | 6 | 7 | 6 | 8 | — | 203 | 71 | 357 |
| | English | 402 | 85 | 252 | 1763 | 272 | 316 | 287 | 18 | 548 | 165 | 4108 |
| | Sanskrit | 4 | 19 | 26 | — | 4 | 4 | 12 | 1 | 72 | 3 | 145 |
| | Hindi | 85 | 117 | 132 | 168 | 61 | 44 | 96 | 47 | 1299 | 223 | 2272 |

in the preceding **Table.** Of the four languages, the number of books in English language covering the ten subject fields is more impressive. Especially on Social Sciences the books in English language is more impressive than the remaining nine subject fields as shown in the preceding **Table.** During the year 1998-99, the National Library has received 2131 books on Social Sciences in English language followed by 2357 in 1999-2000; 1346 in 2000-01; 1495 in 2001-02 and 1763 in 2002-03.

## BOOKS RECEIVED BY CENTRAL LIBRARY, MUMBAI FROM SOUTH INDIA UNDER DB ACT, 1954

The Central Library, Mumbai is one of the recipients of libraries under DB Act, 1954. During the five year period this library has received from Andhra Pradesh 165 books in 1998-99 followed by 284 in 1999-2000, 305 in 2001-2001, 219 in 2001-2002 and 417 in 2002-03 totaling 1390 books in five year period. Likewise from Tamilnadu, the Central Library, Mumbai received 1664 books in 1998-1999 followed by 2281 in 1999-2000,417 in 2000-2001, 2400 in 2001-2002 and 1775 in 2002-2003 totaling 12291 books in the five year period. From Karnataka, the Central Library, Mumbai received 619 books in 1998-99 followed by 215 in 1999-2000, 372 in 2000-2001, 276 in 2001-2002 and 387 in 2002-2003 totaling 1869 books during the five year period. The State of Kerala contributed 176 books during the year 1998-1999 followed by 580 in 1999-2000, 296 in 2000-2001, 112 in 2001-2002 and 417 in 2002-2003 totaling 1581 books during the five year period to the State Central Library, Mumbai. The following **Table** reflects these figures.

**Table : Number of books received by Central Library, Mumbai from South India under DB Act 1954**

| *Name of the State:* | *1998-1999* | *1999-2000* | *2000-2001* | *2001-2002* | *2002-2003* | *Total:* |
|---|---|---|---|---|---|---|
| Andhra Pradesh | 165 | 284 | 305 | 219 | 417 | 1390 |
| Tamilnadu | 1664 | 2281 | 4171 | 2400 | 1775 | 12291 |
| Karnataka | 619 | 215 | 372 | 276 | 387 | 1869 |
| Kerala | 176 | 580 | 296 | 112 | 417 | 1581 |

***Source:*** *Central Library, Mumbai*

The language wise break-up of figures pertaining to the five year period received by the Central Library, Mumbai from the four Southern States is presented in the following **Table.** The library has received more number of books in Tamil followed by Kannada, Malayalam and Telugu.

**Table : Yearwise / Statewise / Language wise Receipt of Books Under DB Act, 1954 by the Central Library, Mumbai from South India**

| Year | Name of the Library | Telugu | Kannada | Tamil | Malayalam | Urdu | English | Sanskrit | Hindi | Others | Total |
|---|---|---|---|---|---|---|---|---|---|---|---|
| | Andhra Pradesh | 77 | – | – | – | – | – | – | – | 88 | 165 |
| 1998- | Tamilnadu | – | – | 1632 | – | – | – | – | – | 32 | 1664 |
| 1999 | Karnataka | – | 260 | – | – | – | – | – | – | 339 | 619 |
| | Kerala | – | – | – | 129 | – | – | – | – | 47 | 176 |
| | Andhra Pradesh | 139 | – | – | – | – | – | – | – | 145 | 284 |
| 1999- | Tamilnadu | – | – | 2163 | – | – | – | – | – | 118 | 2281 |
| 2000 | Karnataka | – | 215 | – | – | – | – | – | – | 66 | 281 |
| | Kerala | – | – | – | 296 | – | – | – | – | 88 | 384 |
| | Andhra Pradesh | 229 | – | – | – | – | – | – | – | 76 | 305 |
| 2000- | Tamilnadu | – | – | 3839 | – | – | – | – | – | 332 | 4171 |
| 2001 | Karnataka | – | 293 | – | – | – | – | – | – | 79 | 372 |
| | Kerala | – | – | – | 296 | – | – | – | – | 88 | 384 |

| *Year* | *Name of the Library* | *Telugu* | *Kannada* | *Tamil* | *Malayalam* | *Urdu* | *English* | *Sanskrit* | *Hindi* | *Others* | *Total* |
|---|---|---|---|---|---|---|---|---|---|---|---|
| | Andhra Pradesh | 144 | – | – | – | – | – | – | – | 75 | 219 |
| 2001- | Tamilnadu | – | – | 2400 | – | – | – | – | – | 252 | 2652 |
| 2002 | Karnataka | – | 156 | – | – | – | – | – | – | 1200 | 276 |
| | Kerala | – | – | – | 112 | – | – | – | – | 86 | 198 |
| | Andhra Pradesh | 125 | – | – | – | – | – | – | – | 292 | 417 |
| 2002- | Tamilnadu | – | – | 363 | – | – | – | – | – | 75 | 438 |
| 2003 | Karnataka | – | 1700 | – | – | – | – | – | – | 83 | 1783 |
| | Kerala | – | – | – | 304 | – | – | – | – | 54 | 358 |

***Source :*** *Central Library, Mumbai.*

# 8

# Conclusions and Suggestions

Legal deposit and Bibliographical organization and control is one of the important aspects of a Country, wherein its intellectual output in the form of books and other reading materials and non-book materials is systematically identified, recorded and made available to the present and future generations. The earliest instrument in this endeavor is the enactment of Press and registration of Books Act (1867). This is one of the earliest acts to be put on the statute book during the British Colonial rule to have control over the printing presses and publications emanating from various parts of the Country. This act provided some sort of bibliographical control over publications emanating from various parts of the country.

From among the four Southern States, Andhra Pradesh has a separate office of the Registrar of Publications to over see the working of this Act. In Karnataka it is Office of the Dept. of Public Libraries, which oversees the working of this Act. In Tamilnadu and Kerala there is no separate establishment to oversee the working of PRB Act, 1867. The job of overseeing the working of the Act and receipt of publications as per the provisions of the Act is entrusted to the Departments of Information and Public Relations of the two States.

Among the four Southern States viz: Andhra Pradesh, Tamilnadu, Karnataka and Kerala, the implementation of the provisions of the Act is more satisfactory in Andhra Pradesh, satisfactory in Karnataka and least satisfactory in Tamilnadu and Kerala.

Legal deposit in India has its genesis with the enactment of delivery of Books and Newspapers (Public Libraries) Act, 1954 by Government of India to have a system which ensures the preservation of Country's documentary heritage. The said act ensures total coverage, through compulsory deposit, of copy of every book and newspaper published in the country at the National Library, Kolkata and the three designated libraries viz: 1. Connemara Public Library, Chennai; 2. State Central Library, Mumbai, and 3. Delhi Public Library, Delhi.

It can be said that not more than 30% to 40% of the books published in the Country are deposited at the National Library, Kolkata. The reason for this State of affairs is lack of cooperation and commitment on the part of publishers. The provision of DB Act, 1954, is mostly implemented in breach. There are several reasons for non-compliance of provisions of the act by the publishers. The important reasons pointed out by the experts have been presented under subsection "Receipt of Books at the National Library" in Chapter-6.

As per Section-3 of the DB Act, 1954, Government of India has designated three libraries viz. 1. Connemara Public Library, Chennai, 2. State Central Library, Mumbai, and 3. Delhi Public Library, New

Delhi as recipient libraries to received a copy each of the publications emanating from the country. It is a fact that the National Library, Kolkata has received more number of books during the five year period under study than the three designated recipient libraries. Of the three designated libraries, Delhi Public Library has been receiving more number of books than the remaining two designated libraries.

It is further revealed that the annual receipt of books at the National Library during the five year period was higher than the three designated recipient libraries. But even this higher receipt of books by the National Library is only one third of the total books published annually in the Country.

It can be concluded that from among the Southern States, the receipt of books from Tamilnadu at the National Library is higher than the remaining three States. The reason for this positive aspect may be the designation of Connemara Public Library as one of the recipient libraries as per Section 3 of the DB Act, 1954. Another reason which may be attributed is that the Publishers inTamilnadu are aware of the provisions of the DB Act, 1954 and conscious of their obligation to send a copy of every publication to the National Library and of course to the other three designated recipient libraries.

India is perhaps the only Country where documents are published in largest number of languages. Of the twenty two scheduled languages in the constitution of India thirteen fall in the Indo-Aryan branch of Indo-European family. Four languages viz. Telugu, Tamil Kannada and Malayalam belong to the Dravidian family with rich heritage of language and literature. It is revealed that from among the four South Indian languages, publications in Tamil occupy the prime position followed by Kannada, Malayalam and Telugu. Publications in Tamil language are far ahead of the other three languages.

The National Library has received more number of Publications in Tamil language (13,241) followed by Kannada (3688), Malayalam (2532) and Telugu (2236) during the five year time frame.

Among the other non-South Indian languages the national library received books in English, Hindi and Urdu and Sanskrit. Books in English occupy the top position totaling (30668) followed by Hindi (9700), Urdu (1331) and Sanskrit (561) during the five year period.

During the five year period 1998-99 to 2002-03, the National Library has received books covering broad subject fields such as: Generalia, Philosophy, Religion, Social Sciences, Linguistics, Sciences, Technology, the Arts, Literature, History and Geography in all major Indian languages. It is revealed that from among the South Indian Languages, Tamil literature occupies the top position followed by Telugu, Kannada and Malayalam literatures.

In addition to these four South Indian languages the National Library has received books in other languages such as: Urdu, English, Sanskrit and Hindi covering the ten broad subject fields. It is revealed that books in English language on the ten broad subject fields are more impressive than the other Indian languages. Especially in Social Sciences, books on English language are more impressive than the remaining subject fields.

Effective and comprehensive national or regional bibliographical control involves production of current national / regional bibliography on a regular and continuous basis and also by bringing out retrospective national regional bibliographies of books received at the national and library / State Central Libraries / designated depository libraries.

*Indian National Bibliography* (INB) has been conceived as an authoritative bibliographical tool of current Indian Publications in fourteen major languages of India received at the National Library, under the provisions of DB Act, 1954. It started as a quarterly in the year 1958 and become monthly in 1964. Right from it genesis in the year 1958, it was not able to meet the expectations of the library profession to have comprehensive and satisfactory coverage of publications emanating from India. It was found that approximately 35% to 40% of the books received from the National Library at the Central Reference Library, the parent body which brings out INB. The National Library itself is receiving about 35% to 40% of total Indian Publications. Besides, the National Library on its part may have excluded a number of publications from accessioning. The INB has set out its own criteria for non-inclusion of certain publications into its fold. Therefore, non-inclusion of about 65% of the receipts affects the comprehensiveness, utility and dependability of INB as a current national bibliographical tool.

INB includes publications of fourteen major Indian languages. It was revealed that from among the four South Indian languages, the coverage of books in Tamil language is more comprehensive than the remaining three languages viz. Telugu, Kannada and Malayalam. The coverage of Telugu language publications in INB is most discouraging. During the five year period i.e. 1999-2003, only 1295 books were included in the INB, when compared with 6346 books in Tamil, 3139 in Kannada and 2069 books in

Malayalam.

It was felt by the authorities of INB that local and individual needs of linguistic States can be met by bringing out separate annual bibliographies of books in Indian languages in the script of respective languages. In the year 1959 the then Ministry of Scientific and Cultural Affairs, Government of India in cooperation with the respective State Governments initiated action of printing and publication of language bibliographies. It can be stated that not much progress has been achieved in this regard. Right from the year 1959 the progress of publication of language bibliographies in the four South Indian languages is not encouraging. During the past four decades 31 annual volumes were published in Malayalam followed by 29 in Kannada, 22 in Tamil and 20 in Telugu. From 1990's the publication of language bibliographies has been stopped.

## SUGGESTIONS

The Press and Registration of Books Act (1867) is one of the earliest Acts which enabled to have for the first time a sort of bibliographical control of Indian Publications. But in reality the Act is not properly implemented in the Country. In South India, except in Andhra Pradesh and Karnataka, there is no separate office or authority to take care of the working of the Act. For effective implementation of this Act; the cooperation and coordination of the Governments such as Home Department, Commercial Taxes, Municipal Administration, Panchayat Raj and the District Collectorates is very essential.

There is a common bond between the Press and Registration of Books Act (1867) and Delivery of Books and Newspapers (Public Libraries) Act, 1954. There is need for the amalgamation of the provisions of the two Acts and elimination of overlapping provisions to ensure implementation of the provision more efficient and less burdensome to the Printers, Authors and Publishers as the case may be.

At present as per the provisions of PRB Act (1867) a Printer has to send three copies of each publication to the Registrar of Publications or any other designated authority of each State. Likewise as per the provisions of DB Act (1954) every Publisher has to send four copies of each publication to the National Library and the three designated libraries in the Country. Together a printer / publisher have to submit seven copies of each publication at their own cost. Therefore, many Printers / Publishers are not sending their publications as per the provisions of the two Acts. Therefore, there is an urgent need for comprehensive legal deposit act for the Country in place of the present PRB Act (1867) and DB Act (1954) and reducing the submission of copy of each publication to the maximum of three to four copies. This measure, it is felt, will improve the receipt of books at the National Library and the three depository libraries.

As it is the scope of the term 'Publication' may be widened in the context of D. B. Act, 1954 to include digital and other electronic versions of reading materials. In addition to print media, audio-visual materials, music cassettes, video-cassettes should also come under the purview of legal deposit.

The Penal Clause under the DB Act, 1954 is to be made more rigorous by increasing the fine for default from Rs.50.00 to Rs. 1000.00 or five times the cost of the book whichever is higher.

The Publishers (and in the case of PRB Act, 1876,

the Printers) may be freed from the obligation of sending books to the depository libraries at their expenses. The National Library should have provision to meet the postal expenses incurred by the Publishers.

The procedure for trial of offence under the DB Act, 1954 may be simplified and the procedure of summary trial under CrPC may be adopted. There should also be provision for designating a number of officials to launch prosecutions against the defaulting publishers.

Due publicity be given through the mass media like the Press, Radio and Television about the provisions of the DB Act, 1954 and also PRB Act, 1876 and the obligation of the Printers / Publishers to deposit copies of their publications to the designated officers in the case of DB Act, 1954, to safeguard the country's documentary heritage to the present and future generations.

There is an urgent need to review the working of PRB Act, 1867 and more so of DB Act 1954 which was in operation for the past five decades. Some of the provisions of the DB Act, 1954 have lost their relevance due to changing information environment in the Country. The Dept. of Culture, Government of India should appoint a review committee / working group to review the working of DB Act 1954 and recommend suitable amendments for its effective implementation in the years to come.

The National Library and the designated depository libraries should conduct awareness programs among the publishers at regular intervals so as to seek their support and cooperation for effective implementation of the Act. The National Library has been organizing seminars / workshops on DB Act, 1954 at important Centers in the Country to create awareness among the Publishers, Authors and the general public. These should be organized frequently at important educational and publication centers in the Country.

There is no authoritative and official agency at the Central Government or among the State Governments which can provide reliable and authentic statistics about the publishing activity in the Country. The data provided by the National Library is not truly reflecting actual number of books published in the Country annually. It provides figures pertaining to books received under DB Act, 1954. These figures do not reflect the actual publication output of the Country. Like wise the data provided by he Registrars of publications / Departments of Information and Public Relations of State Governments which receive publications under the provisions of PRB Act, 1867 do not reflect the actual number of books printed / published in the country as a whole or within the State.

The Central Statistical Organization, Government of India also does not collect statistics on Book Publishing in the Country. Even the Federation of Publishers and Book Seller's Associations in India is not able to provide correct figures pertaining annual book production in India. In these circumstances, it is rather difficult to arrive at correct figures of annual production in the Country. The Central Statistical Organization, Government of India may be entrusted with the responsibility of collecting statistics on annual book production in the Country with the support and cooperation of State Governments.

Comprehensive legal deposit and Bibliographical Control can be possible with the effective implementation of PRB Act 1867 and DB Act, 1954.

The brining out of INB regularly and comprehensively will go a long way in realizing the cherished goal of National Bibliographical Control. Likewise the bringing out of language bibliographies at the State level will ensure in realizing Regional Bibliographical Control (RBC). Towards this end, the role of Registrar's of Publications / Departments of Information and Public Relations / State Central Libraries and lastly but not the least the National Library and the three depository libraries cannot be over emphasized. These institutions should be strengthened in terms of infrastructure, finances, qualified staff and introduction of information and communication technology in the management of these institutions.

To conclude, the role of Department of Culture, Government of India is very crucial to have an effective National Bibliographical / Regional Bibliographical Control of Indian Publications. It has to extend full support and cooperation to those institutions concerned with location, identification, processing, retrieval and dissemination of knowledge / information embodied in documents emanating from various parts of Country.

# INDEX